The Family Shadow

THE FAMILY SHADOW

Sources of Suicide and Schizophrenia

David K. Reynolds and Norman L. Farberow

University of California Press

Berkeley   Los Angeles   London

University of California Press
Berkeley and Los Angeles, California

University of California Press, Ltd.
London, England

Library of Congress Cataloging in Publication Data

Reynolds, David K
  The family shadow.

  Bibliography: p. 171
  Includes index.
  1.Mentally ill—Family relationships—Case studies. 2. Suicide—
Case studies. 3. Schizophrenia—Case studies. I. Farberow,
Norman L., joint author. II. Title.
  RC455.4.F3R49   616.85'8445'09   80-22822
  ISBN 0-520-04213-1

Printed in the United States of America

To the unnamed family of this book, whose courage and openness have provided an opportunity to learn more about the life experiences of the suicidal patient after discharge from the mental hospital.

CONTENTS

FOREWORD

Chuck Smith

Time has an uncanny way of dulling the memory for events and especially for people's names and the parts they play in one's life. I was asked by the authors to write this Foreword. I accepted gladly. A writer myself, I jumped at the chance to spread my views on paper much like an artist with his palette. Funny, I was thinking about the same thing when David K. Reynolds came into my life.

I even forget the season of the year in which we met. I do remember well my sitting in the dayroom of the hospital sipping coffee and watching television. He approached and asked me how I would feel about being shadowed. That's the process of following someone around and keeping notes on his conversations and occasionally bringing out a tape recorder. It didn't take long for David and me to become friendly enough to act like long-time acquaintances. In the dayroom, he explained it to me. He said there were several other candidates for the study. I was most responsive to the offer.

Several days later I learned from David that I had been chosen to be in the study. I felt honored to have so many people interested in my life. The National Institute of Mental Health was sponsoring the project and my parents were to be paid for the researcher's room and board. Soon I was to be discharged from full-time hospital institutionalization to apartment living with my parents.

Dr. Reynolds and I both had cars, but usually I drove mine to the store, to my sister's apartment, and to bookstores and movies. I remember many activities, but I feel the Foreword is no place to include them. They will be in their appropriate places in the book, as will be true pieces of dialogue. I have a funny feeling about the book. One major feeling is that it will bring out certain aspects of my family life which may be a little awkward for us Smiths.

The book is written in the language of psychological or psychiatric anthropology. Some people assume that anthropology means studying decayed ruins and cultures. It was surprising to me the first time I learned of psychiatric anthropology. Well, anyway, the study of stress in the community and the family in private proved to be a good, a very good study. I think we all gained a lot from it. Perhaps you, the reader, will find yourself in my place no matter what your station in life. Studies of life stress are, I believe, becoming one of the most valuable tools for understanding human lifeways. Even before reading the finished book, I can recommend it as highly worthwhile reading for the general audience, not just for the expert or student of anthropology, psychology, and psychiatry.

The following excerpt is from "Me and My Shadow," a patient-newspaper article, by Chuck Smith: "David Reynolds, Ph.D., an anthropologist, spent a month last spring following me nearly everywhere I went. He lived at my parents' apartment with me and my family doing a part of his overall study on stresses related to the outpatient. He took over two hundred pages of notes that will be used in a future book. There was some formality at first, but after a few days, we all began to relax. David soon became 'a member of the family.'"

ACKNOWLEDGMENTS

Our thanks go to Keith Froehlich, M.S.W., and to Joseph T. Crockett, M.D., for helping us in the selection of the Smith family and for arranging initial contact with them. Typing assistance was provided in the main by Majda Andlovec, Mary Guth, Mary Luben, Geraldine Pentheroudakis, and Eleanor Kwong.

Without the courage and openness of this rare family we have chosen to call "Smith," our study would not have been possible. They merit our deep gratitude.

I

INTRODUCTION

Many professionals have observed mentally disordered people in their offices and in other highly structured and artificial settings such as hospital wards and clinic offices. This is where they are most often clustered and most available for study. It is recognized that such settings can provide only limited information and that our subjects are being viewed under highly unnatural conditions that rarely approximate the way they actually live and function. It would be most desirable to observe what happens in their homes while they are going about their everyday activities. At the Central Research Unit of a Veterans Administration Medical Center, we have become interested in this more naturalistic observation and have developed techniques for carrying out such studies in a variety of settings. Beginning in the hospital and then moving from the relative freedom of aftercare facilities to the increased freedom of family life, we have lived with and observed the suicidally and mentally disturbed. These observations have strengthened our conviction that the behaviors of persons labeled "mentally ill" and of persons considered "normal" can be best understood through knowing the physical and sociocultural environment within which the behaviors occur as well as the psychological status of the subjects.

This book reports our observations of a suicidal person who is also schizophrenic in an environment fundamental to understanding his past and present behavior, that is, as he lives with his parents in their home in the community. Funds from a National Institute of Mental Health grant supported arrangements with the patient and his family enabling David K. Reynolds, an anthropologist, to live with them for a month—from the time Chuck was discharged from a psychiatric hospital until he had a relapse and was readmitted. The researcher lived alongside Chuck Smith during nearly all of Chuck's waking hours, recording a view of Chuck's life. The objective was to document the life-style of a suicidal patient treated and discharged from a mental hospital. Prior research (Farberow, Ganzler, Cutter, and Reynolds, 1971) has shown that most suicides of mental hospital patients are by schizophrenics and that most occur off the hospital grounds while the patient is out on pass or soon after discharge. We are, however, poorly informed about such patients when they leave the hospital. We know in general where they go, with whom they live, whether they work, go back to school, or drive a car, but we do not know the pressures, impacts, needs, desires, and motivations that shape their behaviors and reactions.

The present study has sought to fill this gap. In our book, *Endangered Hope* (1977), we examined two environments into which the treated, discharged suicidal patient entered: the board-and-care homes and the family-care homes. We now chose to learn about another major environment: the family in its home. This study held added attraction, for we could observe the subject not only as he reacted to events occurring in the present but also in the context within which he had been reared that had helped fashion him into the kind of person he was now. Chuck and his family generously and, indeed, courageously permitted this intrusion into their private lives and agreed to the publication of this report about the experience. It was their expressed hope that useful discoveries might be shared with other former patients and their families. We believe they also hoped that the researcher's presence would help keep Chuck alive.

The study began with the clearly identified scientific objective of observing a suicidal schizophrenic and his family. How close has it come to its goal? Is such a goal even attainable? There is little doubt that, in the course of living with the Smith family, the anthropologist's vision became selective and distorted. Also, in the time required to write this report, memory may have oversimplified the sketch of these people. Observations have mixed and merged to produce an artistic statement that is, perhaps, too patent and sensible to be trusted as representing reality, unless it be the reality of some sort of documentary novel. The novelist, like all artists, simplifies reality. He can make his characters as complex as he likes, but they act consistently, according to personality themes that the author has created.

The characters feel one emotion at a time—at least the line of print describing their emotions places one feeling word after another. Reality is not like that at all. Feelings at any moment are multiple and complex, and we are each many selves with conflicting and inconsistent traits. The family we describe has no heroes or villains. They appear somewhat simplified and stylized in this book. We have crafted them into symbolic images, as the Smiths did with each other. Believe the symbols if not their images.

Details have been changed to protect the identity of the Smith family. Inasmuch as it is impossible to portray every element of the observed family interaction, we have chosen to emphasize those aspects that we believe relate directly and indirectly to Chuck's suicidality. Changes have occurred since this verbal snapshot was developed. The apartment is different, the family members have grown as individuals, and their interactions have evolved. This report is, then, an historical account of one moment in the thousands of moments lived separately and together in the life of the Smith family.

This study is the third in a trilogy aimed at examining the interactions between subject and settings in which suicides of mental hospital patients occur. In the first project, we used the technique called experiential research to discover some of the precipitators of self-destruction while in the hospital; in the second project, we used the same method to look at the experience in psychiatric residential aftercare facilities. Our experiential researcher (DKR) adopted an alternate suicidal identity and lived in these settings, making observations of his personal responses to the situational pressures of the environments. Full descriptions of these settings and of the experiences in them are given in *Suicide, Inside and Out* (1976) and *Endangered Hope* (1977). In this third report, we describe the lifeway of a family with a suicidal member. Like Jules Henry's book, *Pathways to Madness* (1973), this book represents a pilot effort in the use of anthropological, ethnographic field methods in the study of family culture. Henry's analysis, however, focused on the elements of American culture, sharpening them into patterned foreground as he looked at the behaviors of particular families which produced emotionally disturbed members. Our study takes the cultural background as given and aims at a description of the family world of the Smiths.

From the final discharge procedures at a psychiatric hospital, through a month of family life, to Charles (Chuck) Smith's precipitous readmission to the hospital, DKR lived alongside this suicidal person. With the patient's permission and that of his family, the researcher stayed with him during nearly all of his waking hours, sleeping on the living room floor of the family apartment to be ready to observe and participate in the young man's life from the moment he awoke until the time he went to bed.

In this technique, called "shadowing," the aim exceeded that of the traditional anthropological fieldwork method of detached observation or even the method of participating actively with the subjects in their daily routines. The goal was to approximate as closely as possible the experiential method used in the previous two studies in which the researcher (DKR) adopted the role of a suicidal person and had the advantage of observing his own behaviors and reactions. The goal in this study was to approach a temporary identification with Chuck Smith, to share his world so intimately that, insofar as was possible, the researcher's perspective could begin to coincide or merge with that of his companion.

We recognize, of course, that distances between individuals are immense and ultimately impassable. We acknowledge, nonetheless, the capacity for intense moments of communication, as in feeling the bursting joy of another's success, in sharing overwhelming grief and sorrow at another's loss, in expressing the same words simultaneously, in "knowing" what is going on in the mind of a relative or acquaintance, or in experiencing crowd contagion. Placed in this perspective, the process of momentary empathic identification provides a uniquely revealing insight into our subjects and increases our understanding of the behavior and the relationships of our subjects. It is within these data, derived from both the intuitive-empathic and the objective, that we hope to learn more about how suicide, schizophrenia, and family interact.

Traditional anthropological categories used in the studies of culture, such as kinship, economics, politics, law, education, and religion continue to be relevant in the study of the culture of the family. The above categories may correspond to relationships inside and outside the family, family work and finances, governance and control in the family, rules for family interactions, information exchange, and beliefs and values of the family. Use of these conceptual categories assists the family ethnographer who wishes to avoid major gaps in his description of the family culture. Our field notes were dated and organized into categories that for the most part emerged from the data. In all instances, the researcher attempted to distinguish between (1) "folk" (in this case, "family") interpretations of activities and events and (2) his own interpretations of those phenomena.

The pages that follow include portions of Chuck Smith's hospital records, notes from the researcher's observations of Chuck Smith's daily activities from discharge to readmission, an overview of the literature on suicidal and disturbed families, and an analysis and discussion of those activities and observations.

CHUCK SMITH'S
HOSPITAL RECORDS

The following excerpts have been edited from the medical notes on admission, the nursing notes, the psychology report, and the doctor's progress notes for the four hospitalizations preceding our research.

FIRST HOSPITALIZATION

Medical Examination on Admission

3/4   Twenty-eight-year-old, single, white male. Gives a history of feeling as if "things are closing in on me—Can't get away from this." States he has heard voices for the past year telling him to do things. Has thought of suicide frequently and has made at least two attempts, one with sleeping pills and one with gas. He has had no previous psychiatric hospitalizations and no medical help. Can sleep a lot but still wakes up tired.

Nursing Notes

3/4   Complains of hearing voices and feels as if things are closing in on him. States he has had this condition for approximately one year. Has been unable to work or hold a job for more than a year. Appears well oriented and in good contact. Placed on closed ward.

3/9 Didn't sleep much last night.

3/22 States he is hallucinating. Things are jumping out of the walls at him.

3/24 Patient complains of distorted vision. States many times he see things as either extremely oversized or undersized. States this has developed since his admission.

Psychology Report

Patient comes with complaint of nerves. Describes paranoid ideation, auditory hallucinations; says onset of voices occurred one year ago. Reports feelings of "losing my identity, becoming somebody else." But in talking about his bizarre ideation he manifests a surprising degree of insight; talks about suicidal preoccupation, constant suicidal thoughts; has a history of several suicidal gestures. Diagnosis: Schizophrenic reaction, chronic.

Disposition

Chuck Smith was discharged on 6/30 to a board-and-care home. He was also assigned to an outpatient therapy group.

SECOND HOSPITALIZATION

Eight months after his discharge Chuck made a serious suicide attempt and was again hospitalized. He was treated initially for a gunshot wound with entry on the chest below the nipple and an exit wound posteriorly on the chest. The lung was lacerated. There was blood in the pleural space. A thoracotomy was performed. When his physical condition stabilized he was transferred from the emergency hospital to the V.A. neuropsychiatric hospital.

Mental Status After Transfer

Patient admits to a few suicidal attempts in the last three years after his military discharge. Last year he was admitted to this hospital because of generalized nervousness, insomnia, and auditory hallucinations; he has been on trial visit for the last eight months. Patient sees a doctor once per week and is on Prolixin. Prior to present hospitalization, patient admits to feelings of profound depression. After some discussion with a friend he has known for one year (the friend was also undergoing psychiatric treatment), they both decided to die. According to patient, his friend shot himself and most probably died.

Nursing Notes

3/4   Patient appears drowsy but awake and responding. Placed on intensive care unit. Parents at bedside.

3/6   Visitors here. Patient is talkative . . . joking and talking about school. Very good spirits and appropriate, although he stated to his sister earlier that he was hearing voices that were running his mind. He occasionally stares off into space as if having auditory hallucinations.

3/7   Visited by his family.

3/10   Patient says he was depressed when he shot himself. Brother visiting. Mr. Smith appears at ease.

3/12   The patient appears in good contact. States he had been depressed and was talking to his friend about killing himself. He decided to do so, bought a gun, waited five days, and made the attempt. He says he is glad now that it failed. Feels he learned a lesson. Next time he will find someone to talk to, to prevent becoming so depressed. He has had visits from his parents. Remembers every day since the incident. He feels his family is very supportive of him at this time.

3/14   Patient appears to be in good spirits. States he went to church. "I had a lot to be thankful for."

3/15   Patient was seen in admission staff this morning. He expressed to staff that he will not try suicide again and that when he does become depressed he will ask someone for help. States he has plans for a job in Pasadena.

3/29   Patient met with me for the first time on a one-to-one basis. Our discussion today dealt with his relationship in earlier years between his father, mother, brother, and sister. He describes the family situation as a rather poor one—his father was away from home a lot, parents fighting, discipline sometimes delayed one week or longer until his father came home. Only in recent years has the parents' relationship improved, bringing the whole family closer together.

3/30   Our talk today dealt with (1) his job history, (2) his family's attitude toward his being in the hospital, and (3) his hearing voices and what they say to him:

(1) Mr. Smith told me that from 1966 until the present time he has done the following work: He was a disc jockey in a small town in Alabama for five months and quit. Then he was a taxi driver. Following that job he went back to college for one semester, majoring in Fine Arts. He only needs eight units to graduate, he says. He ran out of money and returned to driving a taxi but quit. "I got tired of doing it." Then he was a cook at a hamburger stand, but again quit. "I got confused—I wasn't completing orders." He then came to the hospital for the first admission.

(2) I asked him, "What was your family's attitude toward you while in the hospital?" "Like I have to be handled with kid gloves. I like the attention," he replied. Next I asked, "And since you left the hospital the last time?" He replied, "They treat me like I am normal, so they don't have to give me so much of their time anymore."

(3) Mr. Smith states that the voices say the following things to him: "Don't do that; do *that*." "Don't use that hand; use the other." They call him "stupid," "crazy," "coward," "failure," "bastard," and "son-of-a-bitch." When asked if he recognized the voices at all, he replied, "Yes, the ones that say 'don't do that; do *that*' sound like my parents. The ones that call me names, I don't recognize."

4/2   Patient left on a weekend pass.

4/6   Mr. Smith appears to present a facade that everything is going well for him. He laughs and smiles at small statements he makes. He expresses a great need for "a true friend." His definition of a true friend is "one you can trust; one who stands by you in any situation; one who gives of himself but wants little in return; one who will admire you in the things you do."

4/9   This morning Miss Brown and I met with the patient and discussed my terminating with him. He appeared to accept this well and voiced the desire to meet with someone else.

4/12   When asked how he would cope with his feelings on the outside, he replied, "I think I'll be able to talk to someone now when I first start getting depressed and not keep it a secret." The staff made the decision to keep the patient longer for evaluation.

4/19   His new nurse asked how his weekend was. Patient, smiling, stated, "I went out dancing Friday night for the first time in over a year." I asked if he enjoyed it. Patient stated, "Yes, very much. I went to 'The Attic,' and they really had a good band there. . . . Oh (with much pride, patient rose from his chair) I brought something back this weekend from home. I thought you would like to see it." Mr. Smith showed an album to me, smiling. It consisted of pictures of himself and many nice write-ups about his work when he was in college and in the service. From the time he gave me the album, he talked, without ceasing, about the plays he acted in while in college and in the service. He also directed many Shakespearean plays. He talked about his work as a disc jockey and as a reporter. Patient has worked in a variety of fields and he appears talented in each. Mr. Smith stated, "I'm writing an autobiography. When I finish it, I would like for you to read it."

4/20   Mr. Smith discussed his father's drinking all during the patient's childhood. The father would come home from work drunk, and his wife would not let him in the house. Then his father would break down the door. This type of behavior existed in the family until about two years ago. Apparently his mother also drank at times. Patient gave his autobiography to me to read. It consisted mostly of his early childhood life and of the numerous jobs that he had participated in since he entered young adult age. I noted that in his autobiography he didn't mention his sister. When I brought this to his attention, he said, "Oh that's true. I didn't mention her."

4/21   At the beginning of our next session, Mr. Smith was very depressed, twisting his hands, and tense. He told me, "I read this psychology book last night, and it dealt with problems in childhood . . . how the mother is domineering and how she selects things for the child to do." I asked him why he reacted this way to the article. He answered, "I really think it is because my childhood was like the article in the book." Mr. Smith indicated that his mother forced him to go into drama. "She told me she would beat me if I didn't."

4/22   "I have been so shy all my life, I'm just beginning to learn how to communicate with others. I have kept so much repressed in me; all of a sudden I feel like I could talk and talk forever. I really didn't like my sister when she was younger, but I do love her now." "Every decision I have ever made I think, if it's going to hurt someone I won't even do it." Patient told that he is very glad that he is meeting with me and his psychologist. He doesn't recall ever having someone to talk to about personal things, things that he had never dared to breathe aloud before. I asked, "Such things as?" He replied, "My mother domineering, my father a drunkard, my brother never really giving me too much of his time, and jealousy and dislike for my sister." After the patient finished talking he took a deep breath, heaved a sigh of relief, and smiled. I asked, "Why did you keep your dark glasses on all through our session?" Mr. Smith stated, "The glasses are sort of a protective device."

4/23   "I feel so good today," Mr. Smith remarked. It was reported by the occupational therapist that the patient appeared somewhat depressed today. No depression was noted at this time, however.

4/25   Having observed Mr. Smith when he was totally unaware of it, I am convinced that he hears voices. His facial expressions changed, and his lips moved as though he were carrying on a conversation, but I heard no sound coming from him.

4/26   I asked the patient if he heard voices. He said he did and that they had never stopped. I asked, "What do the voices say?" "All kinds of crazy things like 'Mickey Finn is dead'; 'Don't touch *that*, touch *this*'; 'Use your left hand, don't use your right'; and 'Be careful of what you say,' " he replied. I asked Mr. Smith if the voices ever went away. "The only time I don't hear them is when I'm talking with someone, and even then sometimes I hear them."

Doctor's Progress Notes

3/18   Our consultant on suicide gave his opinion that this patient is a high suicide risk based on consideration of the circumstances of the recent suicide attempt.

Disposition

Chuck was discharged to outpatient status exactly one year after his first discharge date. He managed to stay out of the hospital for about eight months, as before. His third hospitalization also occurred in May.

THIRD HOSPITALIZATION

Medical Examination on Admission

This patient is a mildly overweight white man in his thirties, dressed casually. He admits he dislikes "being closed in." He says that he was adjusting to life in the community until three weeks ago when "the voices started tormenting me and giving me contradictory orders. Because of the voices it would take me a long time to do anything. Last night I saw the devil. He was after me. I decided to come back." Patient claims that he was hearing the voice of God, Jesus Christ, or Moses. During the interview situation he stated that he heard some sound come from his head, stating that it was the sound of a wolf. Mr. Smith complains of insomnia, and his appetite was quite poor just before he came to the hospital. The main thing that disturbs him about his mother is that she is domineering and quite pessimistic. Diagnosis: Schizophrenia, paranoid type.

Nursing Notes

3/28   Mr. Smith was readmitted. He states he started having difficulties sometime after he stopped taking medication. He feels he was doing okay in the community until about three weeks ago. He didn't appear depressed at first, but after some conversation it was apparent that he is extremely depressed and dejected but puts on a great facade. He is hearing voices that are sometimes complimentary and sometimes derogatory. These began when he stopped taking his medication. He had been working at a food-processing facility. His mother was a supervisor there. When she left he continued to work in the facility and became depressed. I asked, "Who suggested that you stop taking medications?" "My mother, and then what the voice says reinforces the thought of stopping."

4/1   Patient states he still hears voices occasionally but doesn't remember what they say. He appears preoccupied. He doesn't really know what he wants to do. He might return to school. "I'm afraid to in a way because I got F's when I didn't indicate I was dropping out—I just didn't go." Mr. Smith was visited by his mother and father. He didn't have much to say to them.

4/2   When told he had a cake brought by his mother, he said,

"I don't want any of it. Give it to anyone you like." When given the cake after supper, he shared it with some patients.

4/14   Mr. Smith feels very close to his sister. He was at one time close to his brother, but this changed as they went their separate ways. He feels his depression started when he was a sophomore in college. In school, he ran around with a weird group and drank quite heavily until it became a problem with him. If he fears a depression, he selects faster and more lively music to get himself out of the depression.

4/14   The patient states he is not interested in returning to work. Says he is writing a book which he hopes to have published.

4/15   Talked a great deal about his mood music [This was actually Moog synthesizer music. DKR] again. Played some of it on the phonograph. It sounded to me like something out of a horror movie.

4/16   Mr. Smith talked about bugs that were flying around the room. "They continually fly in circles going nowhere. They often do something, mate in the air, and then the male either dies or the female kills him."

4/20   Some of the voices this patient hears are mean and aggressive. They tell him, "Don't put out that cigarette *here*; put it out over *there*." He feels he must rebel and puts the cigarette out on the floor.

4/21   Mr. Smith feels he reacts to others in every way that will make him most "popular."

4/21   Mr. Smith points out that he is growing a beard. Smiles and says it is to "look like Sigmund Freud." Complains of hearing voices "good and bad."

Disposition

Shortly afterward, Chuck was again discharged but within a few months he was back in the hospital.

FOURTH HOSPITALIZATION

Medical Examination on Admission

The patient is a 30-year-old white male veteran, single, nonservice connected. He was readmitted to the hospital from outpatient status on August 14 because of increasing severity of auditory hallucinations, depression, and nervousness.

The patient has a history of previous psychiatric hospitalizations. He has been coming to the hospital every week attending the weekly outpatient meeting and he has been doing fairly well. He has been staying with his parents, applying for a job at the van and storage company where his sister and father work. Meanwhile, he has been writing a book about himself. The hallucinations started getting bad about a week before hospitalization. His medications were adjusted, and this helped him temporarily. Then, about a week ago, he started complaining about the hallucinations increasing again. He became quite depressed. His physical condition is essentially normal. Diagnosis: Schizophrenia, paranoid type.

Nursing Notes

8/14   Mr. Smith was readmitted, accompanied by his mother. Patient complains of depression and hallucinations. He hears voices calling him dirty names. He states that he does not do anything at home except watch TV. Says he has been writing his autobiography.

8/14   Said he came back because he was not feeling well. He had been hearing voices telling him what to do and what not to do. Appeared in good contact, however, and socialized very well. When I asked him to cut his long hair and beard he refused.

8/20   This patient stays close to staff. Appears less depressed and preoccupied today. Visited by relatives and appears happy with them.

8/21   Appears about the same. Presents himself as if nothing is bothering him. Talks only in generalities. States he only came to the hospital for a medication change. Asked if he had been working. "No." Asked what he had been doing. "Only going to the movies and to the beach." What else? "Working on my book all the time." In group therapy, the rest of the patients reacted negatively to this man who doesn't want to work, who only wants to write his book.

8/22   Assigned full privileges card.

8/24   Attends group meetings, but Mr. Smith will not say anything unless a question is directed to him. Appears quite irritable when asked if he is going to have a haircut. Patient is not particularly interested in his grooming at this time.

8/25   Appears to be in high spirits this morning. Patient could profitably lose some weight. He is continually gaining rather than losing.

8/26   Visited by family. The patient appeared to enjoy this visit.

8/27   Visited by parents this evening. Appeared happy during the visit.

8/29   Appears neat and well-groomed. He said, "I felt much better today than last week." He has been talking with an outpatient. "He is my friend. . . . He listens to my problems." He said that he is going to try to get out of his shell. "Well, it's really hard to change our attitude. I've been like this all my life."

8/30   Mr. Smith spoke of himself to social worker as a "nothing."

8/31   Patient very quiet and appears somewhat depressed.

8/31   Complaining of cold symptoms, stuffy nose, and cough.

9/1   States cold symptoms have subsided, feels better today.

9/10   Returned from pass in apparently good condition. States that it is his birthday today, "Thirty-one years and over the hill." When he was told thirty-one to forty-one were great years, he said, "I sure hope so."

Summary of Further Nursing Notes

Chuck worked for six weeks in the hospital's radio repair shop, performing his tasks at a high level with minimal supervision. He was conscientious and willing to work. He was neat and clean in his personal appearance. On 10/20 he was transferred to occupational therapy for prevocational testing. During testing he arrived promptly at the appointed times, was friendly and cooperative, listened attentively, followed instructions well. Mr. Smith showed high scores in spelling and low scores in mathematics but showed average ability in performing structured and problem-solving work tasks.

Doctor's Progress Notes

8/30   On Monday this patient said he had been so depressed over the weekend that he had begun thinking about suicide again. "But I'm okay now." Today he seemed quite cheerful. He expressed anger toward the man who sleeps next to him who is "hung up on Moby Dick."

10/3 Last week Mr. Smith finally succeeded in overcoming intense feelings of depersonalization lasting most of the day. He attends five therapy groups. This week he is looking into a job-training course at a nearby V.A. hospital. He spoke realistically about realizing that his writing of a book about himself may remain an avocation. Eventually he wants to study at night school.

10/27 Mr. Smith lost his volunteer companion and is assigned to another. He is still something of a loner but tries to participate in ward groups and activities; always friendly and agreeable. We feel he is making slow but definite progress.

11/15 The auditory hallucinations became worse four days ago and voices were telling him to throw things at people. He started to become unable to discriminate reality from unreality.

11/17 He said yesterday he had been having some of the same feelings during his upset period earlier this week as he had experienced before he shot himself in the last suicide attempt. Says he feels better now.

12/1 Mr. Smith is doing better. He is friendly and socializes well with others. His progress is notable.

12/18 Mr. Smith was seen in the medical clinic complaining of nausea, vomiting, and other epigastric distress. At that time he admitted to drinking heavily. Further tests proved negative. Patient responded to a bland diet.

1/3 He has been doing fine since placed on new medication. The hallucinations have stopped and he has experienced no problems.

1/19 He went on leave of absence for a week and did fairly well. No problems reported. No overt psychosis at present.

1/30 Mr. Smith has made a good adjustment to this unit socially, but he has no reasonable goals. He states he is going to school at a community college starting in February. He is only a few units away from an A.A. in Theater Arts, but he is not taking the necessary course work to complete his degree. Unless he can come up with a realistic plan to separate himself from this hospital, he will have to be transferred. I am afraid that in his particular case we are only reinforcing his institutionalization as opposed to assisting him toward independence.

2/6   I told Mr. Smith about ten days ago I would discontinue individual interviews with him. He is seen by Dr. H. in individual therapy and also attends her group and my group. His planning regarding school was not done with me, but I have pointed out to him that his last near-fatal suicide attempt was made at a time when he was depressed over school failure. I also pointed out he had to leave the radio-television repair detail because he found the work too stressful when he progressed to transistors. He is now planning to take electronics at a community college. The plan to cooperate in Dr. Reynolds's research was discussed in my presence, and I concurred so long as this and possible discharge plans are discussed with Dr. H. first.

TWENTY-FOUR DAYS IN THE LIFE OF CHUCK SMITH

It would be unfair to the Smith family were we to fail to put into perspective the setting for Chuck's return from the hospital. Whatever provoked or precipitated Chuck's symptoms, his disordered behavior had created many worries and practical problems for his family. Inconvenient visits to the hospital, the moving of personal effects from place to place, financial problems, and other difficulties could be clearly attributed to Chuck. But the family was willing again and again to accept him when discharged, to shelter and advise him, to realign their lifestyles so as to behave in ways they thought would be helpful and supportive to Chuck. Time and again their efforts on his behalf would show only temporary results. Another relapse would prompt a new round of upsets in routines and feelings.

AN INTRODUCTION TO CHUCK SMITH

Chuck spoke knowledgeably of psychology and medications. His use of professional jargon and his wide vocabulary influenced the casual observer to overestimate Chuck's intelligence and insight. He had a taste for the offbeat and nontraditional, and he read imaginative fiction and books on psychics and mysticism. His books and records tended to confirm a view of modern culture as bankrupt and artificial. Bob Dylan (played loudly at his sister's apartment, softly in his parents' home) helped Chuck to justify his position of pessimism and retreat from an ordinary working world. But retreat implied rejection of many activities that typically filled the time of those who did not define themselves as mentally ill. Much of Chuck's behavior could be understood as an attempt to pass time with minimal unpleasantness.

Once outside the hospital, Chuck's activity level dropped sharply. He spent major portions of every day lying on the couch or the floor. He dozed now and then, but he was sometimes alert even when he appeared to be asleep. For example, he would respond to the small sounds of the postman downstairs or he would enter unexpectedly into an ongoing conversation, or he would get up soon after his mother had left the apartment. Like his eating habits, sleep showed no regular pattern, but, unlike his eating, it was never skipped for long. Tranquilizers and coffee (five cups by 1:45 on a typical day) helped keep him in a state of semiawareness. In view of his naps and his lack of exercise, it was not surprising that Chuck had trouble sleeping at night.

The mornings dragged by slowly for Chuck; afternoons went more quickly. He sometimes forgot to take medication at noon. Reading helped to keep at bay Jewel's attempts to control him and served to present the image that he was occupied. Music also eased away the hours. The melodies were enriched by his memories of lyrics and the routines of dancers at the nude bar. Delivery of mail was a big event. Long talks with his mother and an occasional errand or outside activity helped round out his day. Chuck attended a community college in the evening for three hours per week and studied for a couple of hours in preparation for the class.

Chuck accomplished many of his daily activities while lying down. There was much unscheduled, unfilled time. Chuck's life was geared to reacting, to responding to small variations in circumstance, such as picking up his glasses from the optometrist or doing the laundry. Chuck, like his mother and sister, sometimes made activity plans, then simply forgot them. He was helpful to the family when asked, but he rarely initiated a service. One week he did not bathe between Monday afternoon and Thursday morning.

The young veteran seemed to interact easily with Donna's boyfriend, with a door-to-door salesgirl, and with shopkeepers. He was indistinguishable from other customers at the bank, gas station, optometrist's office, bowling alley, movie, or on a fishing boat. He had some insight into anger and depression on both theoretical and personal levels. He was reasonable even when his mother was not, and he had a genuine sense of humor that enabled him to laugh at himself as well as at the world around him.

Money was sometimes spent carefully, sometimes impulsively. He carried $50 in his wallet for several days, but as the money dwindled away, he became more and more eager to return to the hospital. He was humming as he packed to return, calling it "the best hotel in town," but his attitude about the hospital was more ambivalent than such a glib statement would indicate.

What did Chuck think about suicide, depression, and mental illness in general? He believed that some people are more sensitive than others, and that these people can be driven crazy if someone finds a weak spot and picks at it until they crack. But he also believed that mentally disturbed persons collude somewhat in beginning their difficulties, and that they must decide for themselves to get well. He agreed with an author who wrote that people become depressed when they lose interest in life.

With a history of several serious suicide attempts, one might think Chuck took his life lightly. Not at all. He said that once he had almost been killed while sliding down a snowy mountain, so he had concluded that skiing was too hazardous for him. He feared freeways. He considered it a miracle that people live as long as they do, in the light of contamination and pollution.

We contacted Chuck Smith during his final days in the hospital. We were seeking a Caucasian male with a history of a serious suicide attempt who would be discharged to his spouse or parents in the Los Angeles area. Chuck fit the criteria perfectly. In addition, he was about the same age as the shadowing researcher, and they had similar training in the fine arts, similar religious backgrounds, and somewhat similar family structures (both with living parents and younger sisters). Those similarities would facilitate the empathic identification of the live-alongside investigator. A meeting with the family was arranged, and signed permission was obtained from Chuck and his parents to permit Dr. Reynolds to live with them, to take notes, and to publish relevant material. Of course, the researchers agreed to protect the family's anonymity (see Appendix A).

THE SMITH FAMILY

The family to which Chuck was discharged had four other members, although Chuck would be living with his mother and father only. At this time, a brief introduction to each family member is in order, as is a preliminary assessment of the household's ambience.

An elder brother, on the police force, was married (with children) and lived far enough away to make his visits family events. Chuck saw Leon only once during the month of our research, although they talked on the telephone a couple of times.

Donna, Chuck's younger sister, lived in an apartment within walking distance of the parents' apartment building. A secretary and a devotee of sports and travel, Donna had achieved an intermediate level of independence from her parents—less distant than Leon, less attached than Chuck. She provided Chuck with healthy support and a place to get away from the pressures of the parental household.

Chuck's father, Charles Smith, Sr., once had a serious drinking problem. At the time of our study he had been dry for years and had achieved recognition as a respected dispatcher in a moving company. He had a tough, caustic wit and an ability to interact without being "involved." His was the ultimate formal authority in the family, but he had to alternate aggressiveness and distance to maintain this position.

Chuck's mother, Jewel Smith, was clearly the dominant figure not only in Chuck's life but in the whole family's. Each family member had to develop some means of coping with Mrs. Smith's strong need to control. She had wit, a fine sense of humor, and no little insight into her tendency to dominate. Nonetheless, hers was the *force* that moved the family. DKR's journal presents a story of Mrs. Smith at least as much as it presents a tale of her son.

Broadly speaking, this was a close family that shared affection freely with many verbal expressions and unselfconscious embraces. Some secrets and deceits were maintained, as in any family, along with an element of aggressiveness and battle, only partially softened by jokes and clever repartee. There was no extraordinary self-consciousness in the Smith household about death or insanity. Utterances such as "I'd go crazy trying to figure this out" or "You may think I'm crazy to . . . " passed unnoticed. Once, Mrs. Smith spurted in indignation as Chuck stood in her way, "Are you crazy or something?" Chuck remarked as he showed me two burned holes in his shirt, "I must be nuts for smoking."

The major dynamics of this family's interaction centered around the mother's control. Each member had to adjust to that key phenomenon. Chuck reacted by withdrawal, avoidance, and intellectual nit-picking; Mr. Smith responded with dry humor and (rarely) an aggressive stand. Chuck and his father both used passive resistance, delaying tactics, and physical distance in their attempts to avoid

Jewel's control. Donna, the daughter, employed confrontation and demand requests of her own.

A shadowy miasma permeated the parents' living room. Perhaps it represented the phantom of past cruelty, or the phantom of daily struggles for control, or the phantom of Jewel's concealed depressions, or the phantom of Chuck's suicidality. This shadow clung to the researcher, coloring his journal pages and his file cards of observational notes, making their editing a depressing prospect. Its significance may become apparent in the pages of this book.

Other characters appear now and again in the journal: friends, hospitalized and recently discharged, hospital staff, local shopkeepers, a mechanic, a salesperson, and hostesses in a bar. The anthropologist observer will make himself known as well, giving some sense of his interaction with Chuck and of their impact on one another's lives.

THE JOURNAL OF A FAMILY SHADOW

The following journal observations, edited by DKR from his notes, record the daily existence of Chuck Smith during one month between his discharge and readmission to the psychiatric hospital.

February 20, Tuesday

Morning.

  7:45 Chuck got up, dressed, and ate breakfast. He stripped his bed and took the sheets to the hospital laundry room. No one spoke about his leaving today. He weighed himself and measured his height (214½ lbs. and 5 ft. 10 in.) Though he had once been athletic in build, his weight now hung on hips and abdomen.

  7:55 Chuck cleaned out his locker.

  8:10 He went to the ward secretary for a check-out slip. "It'll be a few minutes." She wondered whether or not he was supposed to get a clearing slip from another ward.

  8:20 Mr. D., an aide, had not written the transfer note.
        "For this one?"
        "Mmm hmm. . . ."

Chuck: "This my chart?" "Yes." "A lot of paper in it."
The folder was thick with notes from four admissions.

8:35 Chuck was still waiting. But then, that was not unusual for a
small frog lying on the bottom of the pond.

8:40 Staff and patients began to take notice that he was leaving:
"The best of luck to you."
"Come back and see us sometime."
"Good luck, Chuck. Watch out."
"I'm going home today. . . ." "That's good, Smith."
"I like your beard."
"How do you feel about today?" I asked him.
"I feel like I'm graduating from high school. I'm going
out into the community. What am I going to contribute?"
He sounded like a valedictorian. I hoped we'd get past
that stage.

8:55 He was asked if he were an outpatient, service connected.
"Not service connected," he replied. "Not service connected?" "No." But the clerk checked his record anyway,
giving no acknowledgment that Chuck had been right all
along.

9:20 Someone remarked that the discharge procedures were "taking extra long today." Staff and patients wandered by and
greeted him. "I'm leaving today." Chuck made sure they
knew.

9:30 His doctor, social worker, nurse, and nursing assistant were
present for Chuck's final staffing. He was asked his plans. He
told them he was planning to go to school and would spend a
lot of time reading. Did he have sufficient medication? Yes,
enough for three weeks or more. He was asked if he would
continue coming to the group meetings on Thursdays. He
would. Through those meetings they could keep track of his
progress and any problems he might have. "Give my regards
to your family." The psychiatrist pulled his chair back.
"Okay." The meeting was over. "Good luck."

10:05 Signatures accumulated on the check-out slip. Chuck
scrounged grocery bags for packing. He moved leisurely but
purposefully. He had checked out before, more than once.
"That's it," he said, the last signature obtained.

10:30 He finished cleaning out the locker and wiped it with paper
towels.

Afternoon.

1:30   We arrived at his parents' apartment. He told his mother, Jewel, that he was officially discharged. They kissed and began talking about his nieces and nephew, his sister's recent trip, the Los Angeles heat wave, bookstores, and the like. Perhaps for my benefit, they mentioned that Chuck was overprotected. Chuck asked if there were space for me here. In all, it was a safe, settling-in interaction. Now what?

1:45   We emptied the cars, his and mine, and, tired, drank orange juice. Jewel worked at sharpening sticks for a rug-weaving project.

"Have you been doing any studying?" his mother asked.

"Not today, I've been busy."

"Anyway, you're probably pooped."

"Not really," Chuck responded.

1:50   Chuck began to read. All was well so far. Time out.

2:10   After praising Leon, Chuck's brother, for his award-winning lifesaving action, Mrs. Smith headed for bed. "If I go to sleep, you be sure to wake me up at three o'clock now."

2:45   Mrs. Smith returned to the living room. She had awakened herself.

3:10   Several times, Chuck commented to his mother on passages from a book he was reading, giving her information that she willingly absorbed.

4:25   Chuck returned from the bookstore. His father, Charles, Sr., and his sister, Donna, had returned from work. Donna smiled and asked easily, "Where's my hug?" Chuck found it for her. Donna's numerous boyfriends were a common topic of conversation in the family. Chuck had no girlfriends at all.

"Do you mind if I have one little piece of the paper?" Jewel, with a subtle rebuke, demanded her share from her husband. "You dummy! Don't forget your mother!" Mrs. Smith exclaimed when Charles started to put back one of the serving plates on the shelf.

5:50   We went shopping, then to Donna's apartment. Chuck had beer and Donna had a mixed drink. Donna made us comfortable, then went about her own business interrupted by numerous phone calls. A variety of record albums, including *Patton, Bill Cosby*, and chamber music, spun around on the phonograph. Chuck made several trips to the corner store for more beer. Well known to the storekeeper, he joked as he picked up a six-pack.

7:30 Chuck stayed "one up" on Donna by virtue of his intelligence and education. Once, when Donna used an elaborate word in her conversation, Chuck challenged, "Where did you learn that word?" "See, I know *one* thing you don't," she replied.

7:50 Donna was picked up by her boyfriend. With minimal sleep the last few nights because of going out so much, she was tired. Still, she went. She gave me the key to her apartment so I could stay there when she was away on a trip. She reminded us to make sure the candles were out and the stereo turned off before we left. A pop radio program pounded its loud rhythms through the apartment for nearly two hours.

9:45 We returned to the family apartment. We ate dessert while watching TV. Arrangements were made for me to sleep on the floor in my sleeping bag.

February 21, Wednesday

Morning.

6:30 Donna called. No one got to the telephone in time to answer, but everyone knew who it must have been.

6:33 Chuck called her back. She had been taking medication to keep awake. Chuck told her to be careful.

6:45 Suddenly a rumble shook the apartment. An earthquake! Chuck thought at first that the vibration was from someone running down the stairs outside. A neighbor ran outside crying. Mrs. Smith stepped to the doorway and joked with another lady. Chuck turned on the radio. Donna called to say that she was all right.

7:00 Mr. Smith left. "I'll try to be careful." "Don't try, just be," responded Jewel. "Bye, Daddy." She worried that a small earthquake might be followed by a large one. We reminisced about earlier earthquakes.

7:55 Jewel exhibited an almost childlike need for recognition. "That's so pretty!" she remarked, praising her own rug-weaving handicraft.

9:05 Chuck went across the street to a liquor store to purchase a money order. He was in no hurry. At home Chuck was not rushed and had adequate money to cover even his whims. The close family interaction was predictable and secure in contrast to the uncertainties facing an ex-patient who is placed in an impersonal board-and-care facility.

The family decided that I was to be considered a third brother. There was still some carefulness and host-guest formality, but it was already breaking down with familiarity. I was welcome to help myself to snacks from the refrigerator, to tear off my own paper towels at mealtime (during my initial days with them, the Smiths did not use napkins), to pour my own glass of water.

9:20 Chuck emptied the wastebaskets. Jewel told me she felt Chuck was "trying" now and she hoped it would last. It was "almost back to like before" (i.e., to the period before he first became disturbed). Perhaps he could even get a job this time, Jewel mused.

9:30 The mail arrived.

9:35 Chuck began to clear the bedroom and to put away the contents of the paper bags. Jewel seemed careful and polite, obviously trying to avoid antagonizing her son. She consciously made efforts to praise him. Chuck in turn seemed to ignore these overtures, resisted prodding, and seemed to take Jewel for granted. He even appeared to be somewhat inconsiderate and insensitive to her feelings in the way children often resist and passively rebel against parents.

11:00 Chuck had his car serviced at a nearby gas station because it was convenient. An acquaintance passed by and paused to exchange a few words with Chuck. There was no clue during the hour there that anything or anyone was "nonordinary."

Afternoon.

12:40 Back home, in response to my question, Chuck told me that some people knew about his psychiatric hospitalization, for example, the acquaintance at the gas station, and others did not know, for example, the liquor store owner.

1:30 I napped. Chuck slept from 1:30 to 4:15 P.M. while soft music was playing on the stereo.

3:00 I talked with Jewel. She told me that when Chuck shot himself it almost killed her. She had no knowledge of Chuck's other suicide attempts or of his having tried various nonprescription drugs. She said that he had had girl trouble while in the service. He had wanted to marry a girl, but Jewel had intervened, not liking the girl at all. At Jewel's request, a mutual friend had obtained information supporting her view that the girl was no good for Chuck. Jewel said that she knew why Donna was popular with boys. Having grown up around older fellows, she had learned how to get along with males almost as if she were one of the boys. Jewel's daughter had had one long relationship that seemed over, although she continued to exchange letters with the young man in Germany. Her breakup with the boyfriend came at Christmas. Jewel reported that Donna confided in her about it. "I'm glad she comes to me to talk to."

His mother had advised Chuck to make acquaintances at his college, but not to make friends yet. Clearly, she wanted Chuck to herself and the immediate family. She expressed some guilt about a past reaction to Chuck's lying around the house. She had prodded him, "Get out and get a job or go to the V.A. hospital for help." That was at the time of his first hospitalization. It is interesting that Chuck remembered the incident differently. He remembered her noticing his nervousness and trembling hands, suggesting that he go to the hospital—a much milder maneuver.

Jewel worried that Chuck might be able to hear our conversation. She also worried that he might have been pressured to come out of the hospital too early. I was broadly supportive in responding to her worries and doubts.

4:25 A neighbor dropped in to chat about the earthquake. He talked mostly with Mrs. Smith. Chuck's father had returned from work. He and Chuck were quietly absorbed in reading.

5:00 Dinner was served.

5:15 While Mr. Smith napped on the couch, we watched television.

6:00 We left for Chuck's class in physiological psychology at a local community college. We had planned to eat dessert before leaving but forgot.

6:30 We arrived early and had a Coke.

7:00 Chuck waited outside for the course instructor so that he could introduce me. Chuck greeted one girl and chatted with two other smokers while waiting. He noticed the pretty coeds and smiled appropriately when I commented on his stereotypical male role behavior.

February 22, Thursday

Morning.

6:40 Mr. Smith was shaving and Chuck was up fixing coffee. Chuck sat, smoking and drinking coffee.

6:55 Mr. Smith left for work.

7:00 Five minutes after her husband left for work, Jewel got up. We talked about vitamins and grocery shopping. Jewel asked about Chuck's plans for the day. He told her that he and I would be going to the 1 P.M. group therapy meeting at the hospital and that we would eat supper there. Mrs. Smith commented that Chuck and his father are quiet and relatively passive. We chatted about television years ago and Chuck's psychology class material, and, finally . . .

8:15 We ate breakfast.

8:30 Chuck studied. Mrs. Smith was in the kitchen. Family members seemed to forget that a topic had been discussed previously and the same facts would come up again and again (e.g., the earthquake, Richter readings, and the discussion of the myelin sheath from last night's class).

8:50 Chuck lay on the couch for five minutes and then got up to get a paperback book.

9:18 "Buddy, your feet stink!" Mrs. Smith said suddenly. "They don't either," Chuck defended himself. "It's the *shoes*." She wrinkled her nose. Chuck said nothing. She switched the subject. His family had not told the car insurance man of Chuck's hospitalization, fearing increased rates. In Jewel's opinion, "We didn't exactly lie to him. We just didn't tell the whole truth." A pause. "Would you rather I didn't talk so much?" Jewel asked. "It's okay," Chuck replied and he rolled over on the couch, turning his back to her.

10:10 Chuck had been sleeping on the couch for a half hour. "I think I'll go take a shower," he announced in delayed response to his mother's earlier criticism of his feet. After he left the room, Mrs. Smith took the opportunity to tell me that Chuck's father and brother used to drink heavily but did not now. She did not mention that she had drunk heavily, too, as Chuck had reported. From her conversation, it was clear that Jewel did not like being controlled (she avoided *scheduled* vacations, found it difficult to take prescriptions at *specific times*). She preferred to control. She spoke of the parents' plan to use this research honorarium to finance a surprise trip for Chuck. She showed me an afghan she had made. "That's for my critical son, Leon. I'll bet he picks at every stitch to see I did it right." She felt she did better on Chuck's afghan—less pressure.

10:55   "I feel like going for a walk, but I don't have any reason to go," Chuck remarked. Mrs. Smith suggested that he get some eggs at Boys' Market. "Too far," Chuck objected. But we went, returning at 11:35 A.M.

11:40   We ate lunch and soon left for the V.A.

Afternoon.

1:00   Fifteen persons attended the outpatient group therapy. Chuck was quiet but alert. He explained my presence straightforwardly to the group. "How do you like it?" one of the social workers asked. "It's kind of fun," was Chuck's response. A disturbance during the meeting was caused by an aggressive patient who had wandered in. He threatened everyone and ranted about patients being overmedicated into a vegetable-like status. His tone was frightening and offensive, but he touched upon an issue with which many patients sympathized.

3:45   We attended Dr. Harrison's group. Five patients and the therapist were present. Chuck considered it all right to be late. My status was explained to the group. Dr. Harrison wanted Chuck to show his book manuscript to me, but Chuck sidestepped her suggestion.

5:35   We went to his old ward. "What do you do all day?" "Study and read." "That's all?" "Yes. Today we went for a long walk, about a mile."

6:00   We left for school. Chuck was supposed to give a ride to an inpatient named Lou, but Lou was not to be found. School was important for Chuck. It seemed to be *the* reason for Chuck's being. School provided a purpose for living and a hopeful future. He was careful not to be late.

Chuck told me that his mother denies his most recent suicide attempt, thinking the other fellow (who died in the suicide pact) may have tried to kill him. She did not know of his other suicide attempts. While eating tacos, we talked about his last suicide attempt. Chuck told me he shot himself and then threw the gun to this friend.

7:00   Chuck participated in class. He seemed alert and absorbed in the instruction.

9:30   As we drove home, Chuck opened a window because of feelings of claustrophobia. He felt smothered otherwise. But he did not consistently open a car window every time he was driving. Under what circumstances was he claustrophobic?

10:00   Back at the apartment there was a message from Donna to call her. She wanted Chuck to pick her up at 5:30 in the morning, then to pick up her boyfriend to take them both to the airport by 6:30 A.M. Jewel objected, "It's always on *our* shoulders. Why can't *his* parents pick him up?" Then she relented, "Well, you can sleep all day Friday." In this regard, Chuck's life-style was very convenient for his family. He was almost always available for errands and for driving them from place to place.

11:00   We went to bed. Jewel sent Chuck out to the living room to look for her robe, but it was not there. She decided she must have hung it in the closet.

February 23, Friday

Morning.

5:00   Donna called, apologized for waking me, and asked if I would wake Chuck and tell him to be over just before 6:00 A.M. That would give him an hour to have coffee and smoke. Chuck was up, dressed, and had his coffee by 5:20 A.M. He read the *TV Guide*. He seemed cheerful.

5:45   We left to pick up Donna. The car window was open. The first radio program news report was that of the suicide of a 25-year-old male who killed himself with a .38 revolver.

There was no visible reaction from Chuck. His driving was careful, and he made no comment about the subject. Chuck and Donna greeted each other with a hug.

6:30 Gil (Donna's friend and companion on this ski trip) arrived. "He's studying me," said Chuck in response to Gil's question about my presence. We left for the airport. Only the window wing was open this time.

Chuck remarked that he was glad for the chance to repay his family by providing transportation in return for the hundreds of trips they made to the hospital when he was undergoing treatment.

7:45 We returned to the apartment. Chuck and Jewel conversed with animation about their past house in Texas—the beautiful front yard, friends sleeping in the back yard, Jewel's cooking for them, Donna's courage and daredeviltry as a child, and the garden.

8:30 After breakfast, Chuck read a book. His mother told him he shouldn't read so much. Later, when he lay down, she said, "It's hard on your eyes to lie down and read." Chuck stays "one up" on her (as on Donna) by virtue of his education. He was careful not to appear to be too obviously under her control. When she gives a direct order or suggestion, he opposes it or waits before obeying.

9:10 Chuck was reading *I Never Promised You a Rose Garden*. To no one in particular, he remarked, "I feel sorry for the families and relatives of people in mental institutions. They all feel guilty that it's their fault those people are in there." Mrs. Smith responded that she and her husband felt that way, too, but they could not figure out what they had done or not done for Chuck. They felt better after talking with the doctor at the hospital.

9:30 Chuck roused himself to mention the possibility of going fishing. Then he went back to reading and napping.

10:15 Chuck talked about the patient who had disturbed our group meeting yesterday. He said that he, too, had entertained some of the same thoughts about medication but had not spoken of them openly. His Prolixin made him dopey at first, but it forced him to rest and settle down. "Now my dosage is so low I can hardly feel it." His mother noted, "Now you can tell ahead of time when the medicine isn't taking effect."

"Yes, I can tell now." "That's good." Jewel learned for the first time that Chuck's medication had been changed twice during his last hospitalization. She shifted the topic to returning POWs who are finding themselves separated and divorced from their wives, remarking "It's such a cruel, selfish world." Chuck took a reasonable, realistic view in such discussions, as if to counteract his mother's pessimism. The women had needs, too, he noted, that accounted for many POW divorces.

10:20 While Chuck was gone for the mail, Jewel exclaimed, "My head is in a pink cloud. He's finally opening up and letting some of this out. He never used to talk about the hospital. I think your being here has helped." "I'm a good listener," was all the response I offered.

10:30 As Mrs. Smith began to prepare lunch, Chuck was lying on the floor reading his mail. She asked for help to saw a ham bone. She paused. "Come on now." Chuck countered, "Just a minute." Jewel responded, "I believe I can do it—oh, I just don't have the energy." Chuck delayed again. "I'll do it." He waited, reading. She went off, then came to sit in the chair. Chuck remained engrossed in his reading. After a few minutes he went in to saw the bone.

11:00 At the laundry, Chuck helped fold some of the dry clothes.

Afternoon.

12:30 In the market, Jewel spoke disparagingly of a fat woman in slacks and of the store's business difficulties. In contrast, she praised herself, then recognized what she was doing and admitted it, as if that excused the matter and finished it.

12:50 Chuck read while lying on the apartment floor. Mrs. Smith wanted to talk. "Why don't you get a book?" Chuck suggested. "Why don't you tell me to shut up?" she laughed. "Because I'm not crude," Chuck retorted.

1:35 Chuck and I went to the Redondo Beach Sport Fishing Pier to inquire about the fishing-boat schedule. On the way back Chuck blew his horn at a driver who was trying to make a left turn from the wrong lane, remarking that he had better get out some of his rage so that it would not turn to depression. He had a wry smile. He had learned this equation of feelings: soured rage becomes depression.

2:55 On to Donna's apartment. After ten minutes and one beer,

Chuck went to sleep on the couch. I slept for about forty-five minutes on the floor. He was awakened by the next-door neighbor who wanted to borrow something of Donna's. This place was a haven from Jewel's talking and constant emotional evaluations.

5:00   With another can of beer and a cigarette, Chuck simply sat at the dining room table.

My influence was complicated in this setting. If I did nothing, I was a model of inactivity. If I took the lead, as I did in postponing the fishing trip, and as I was often tempted to do because of the vacuum of inertia, I became another controller in Chuck's world and an active bias in our study. For the most part, I resisted the urge to lead and developed my patience by exercising restraint. Chuck remarked that his mother is sometimes dishonest with herself. She fears to see herself as she is. He agreed with my interpretation that Jewel uses extremes of evaluation in assessing her world. She sees its aspects as extremely good or bad with little middle ground.

He was somewhat bitter when his mother found and threw away his collection of *Playboy* magazines. He considered them useful sources of short stories and recipes. He considered Jewel to be prudish. Chuck reflected that he could not stand to see someone hurt another person in premeditated fashion. We talked about the price of escape from a hurtful world when escape was into mental disorder. I explained that my research purpose went beyond describing his world. I was trying to see the world as he did. I appreciated his telling me what he was thinking so I could check out my intuitions. I wanted both experiential and intellectual knowledge. At this time, Chuck still had no key to his parents' apartment and occasionally borrowed his mother's. I had a key to Donna's apartment, but Chuck did not.

5:45   Chuck went to the store for another beer and some potato chips. He made no mention of supper. Chuck felt sorry for people in board-and-care homes. He felt less sorry for patients in the hospital. He said that when you leave the hospital, you have to give up many friends. Chuck mentioned his plan to write a letter to his friend in Germany (Donna's ex-boyfriend), probably tomorrow.

6:30 Chuck made a telephone call to an outpatient friend but, since he was not home, he chatted with the friend's girl. I asked if he wanted me to leave. "No, stick around." He told the young lady he was not doing much but was enjoying his freedom. "I think a lot about the hospital and what the guys are doing back there."

6:50 Chuck's friend returned his call and invited him to come over.

7:30 Having picked up beer on the way, we arrived. There were wine, pot, and beer. Chuck played the guitar and the five of us sang. The talk was about suicide, mental hospitals, books, and algebra. At last I ate cheese, crackers, and nuts. We had eaten no supper. Chuck got high and then sick. I drove him home, stopping along the way to drop off his outpatient friend and to pick up mail at my apartment.

9:30 Cold dinner was waiting at his parents' apartment. I ate, but Chuck went straight to bed. Mrs. Smith pumped me for information about Chuck's activities. I admitted only that Chuck had had a couple of beers and that I had driven home.

10:00 I went to Donna's apartment and showered, wrote notes, and went to bed.

February 24, Saturday

Morning.

8:00 Chuck woke up just as I arrived at the apartment. Jewel asked Chuck how he was feeling. "I'm fine."

8:10 We talked, drank coffee, and made plans for the day. Jewel praised Leon's salary, talked about insurance and paying bills. Chuck sat responding in monosyllables.

8:25 Jewel flashed a not-so-subtle hint, "Remember how Bill Quarry used to borrow things all the time? He seemed to think we owed him that. There's a lot of people who think the world owes them a living." She moved to a related subject. Her husband used to loan things out a lot. "He was too freehearted and that got him into trouble." Mr. Smith was still sleeping. Jewel began to prepare breakfast.

8:45 Mr. Smith got up and sat in the living room, drinking coffee and talking of food.

9:05 Chuck's father told Jewel she should not put her coffee cup precariously on the arm of the sofa. She promptly put down *his* attempt to direct *her*—a straight clash, a head-on disagreement. He didn't respond. Chuck was reading.

9:08 Mrs. Smith prepared her husband's breakfast as he read the paper.

9:12 As Mr. Smith was eating breakfast, Jewel joined him. They "fussed" and she quipped, "That's what you get for marrying me." "I'll remember that next time." Chuck continued reading on the couch, not part of the semiaggressive game.

9:20 Father joined son on the couch and read the newspaper.

10:00 Chuck emerged from the bathroom after ten or fifteen minutes. Jewel said, "I missed you, Son. You were in there so long I missed you." "Is that so?"

Afternoon.

1:00 My resolve was not to direct his life, but weakened by hunger, I suggested that we eat. Chuck and I made sandwiches.

1:15 His parents returned with groceries and put them away. They complained of the high food prices. Chuck was reading.

1:30 We went to Donna's apartment and listened to records for the entire afternoon.

5:15 Chuck had more resources and more settings to live in than most people: a large record and tape collection, books, two apartments, friends, school, and the hospital. But staying in the two apartments, reading and listening to records, was already palling for me. Even these resources can be exhausting if overused. Too much leisure and purposelessness seemed to result in boredom and decreased life value.

5:55 Mrs. Smith telephoned. Chuck expected that it was she, since we had already passed the regular time for dinner. "All right, okay," he said. We left for supper.

6:25 Chuck asked if I wanted to see the movie, *Lady Sings the Blues*.

6:30 Mr. and Mrs. Smith were watching news on TV. Chuck was reading.

7:20 There was a knock on the door. Chuck answered it. The next-door neighbor said that he was hosting a meeting and would try to keep the noise down. Mrs. Smith said, "How nice. How thoughtful to let us know."

7:50 Chuck told me we would go to a movie tomorrow because the next show tonight would be starting too late. He moved to lie down on the floor in front of the TV. Mrs. Smith told him not to go to sleep because we would have dessert soon. He told her to wake him up for dessert. She refused. "I will not." Charles, Sr., stretched out on the couch to watch Lawrence Welk. Chuck was soon asleep, but he wakened now and then when Jewel commented about something on television.

8:15 Mrs. Smith got up to serve dessert. Chuck said, "I don't want any." Mrs. Smith said, "Ohhh, sissy." Chuck said, "Sissy?"

February 25, Sunday

Morning.

8:05 "Chuck, be careful. The chair will come all to pieces." Chuck was sitting forward on the chair Jewel had recently recovered. We talked about the book on mental illness Chuck had finished reading last night. I learned that Chuck worked in a sanitarium as an aide during his last year of high school. He had helped to administer shock therapy. At that time he had planned to be a psychologist or an actor. "Do you think you would've been happy with an acting career?" Jewel wanted to know. "You have to be a super egotist to be an actor. My ego isn't that great anymore," Chuck replied.

8:15 Mrs. Smith wanted to get her hair done. She said she would "feel a little bit better. I'm getting into a rut."

9:45 Chuck lay on the couch and read while his mother trimmed the indoor plants.

9:50 Chuck inquired, "Did you take your medicine this morning?" "Yes." "Good." (Mrs. Smith had been forgetting to take her heart medicine at the proper times recently.)

10:05 There was some mildly paranoid talk about someone who jokingly put a Gestapo sticker on the family car while Mr. Smith was away on vacation. "It seems so lonesome without my husband here. (He was sleeping late because he had worked the night before.) I know it's Sunday and he's supposed to be up. You never did tell me if you wanted to go with me to the beauty shop, Chuck." "I think I'll stay here."

10:50 Jewel commented that she used to be a tomboy. She bragged about her skill at hunting, swinging from a rope on a home-made pulley, and driving. She said her brother was a "mama's boy" until her mother died. "Then he had to grow up and be a man like he should." Another message for Chuck?

10:55 Mrs. Smith left. Chuck promptly sat up, lit a cigarette, and stopped reading.

11:00 Soon after taking out the trash, Chuck was back lying on the couch, reading and then sleeping.

Afternoon.

12:50 Mrs. Smith returned and began to heat lunch.

12:55 As his father got up, Chuck awakened. But he continued to lie on the couch.

1:05 Chuck went to pick up a newspaper. Mrs. Smith said, "I sure do miss Donna." Her husband agreed, "I do, too. The phone doesn't ring nearly as much."

1:10 Chuck asked if anybody wanted to read the paper, but no one did at the moment.

Chuck accidentally splashed water on his mother. Startled, she accused, "You did that on purpose!" Chuck denied it. She laughed and said it was cold.

9:50 After the movie, we returned to Donna's apartment. Chuck listened to Bob Dylan records. He drank beer. Suppertime was long past. This nonscheduling of meals fitted in with the nonbusiness of his life. Was Mrs. Smith worried about where he was? Was this a tactic to escape her control? To assert independence? To upset her?

10:40 We returned to his parents' apartment. Chuck had forgotten about dinner. Mrs. Smith called him the most thoughtless person and a dummy. She was peeved that we were late but laughed it off. We prepared our own meal, left out from the parents' supper.

11:15 Chuck sat smoking. He asked if I had found many stresses so far, referring to our project's goal of looking for stresses and positive experiences in an ex-patient's life. So, I fed system-related data back into the system. I told him of potential stresses he seemed to be avoiding by having various settings for living, various groups for interacting, proper medications, sufficient money, interests, escapes, and future-oriented pursuits. I felt that potential problems might lie in the limited constructive activity in which he engages, his mother's controlling orientation, and the lack of physical activity. Such a candid response on my part intruded a potentially strong bias in our study of Chuck's life. The conflict between the detached observer role and the involved helper role was very apparent at this time.

February 26, Monday

Morning.

6:45   Chuck awoke and called me at Donna's nearby apartment as I had asked him to do.

7:00   I arrived at the Smiths' apartment. Chuck was sitting drinking coffee, barefoot, but was otherwise dressed. Mrs. Smith was preparing lunch for Mr. Smith, who was about to leave.

7:15   Chuck remarked that people became robots to protect themselves. He told me of two dreams from the previous night. The first involved flying and LSD. From his elevated perspective in the first dream, he saw clearly that earth (his life) is hell. In the second dream, a curfew man caught Chuck outside after dark and machine-gunned him.

8:20   Referring to her grandchild, Jewel remarked, "He's so strong—mentally." The dimensions of mental strength and weakness were important in her evaluation of people. "Strength" seemed to involve will, assertiveness, perseverance, and fortitude, but not intelligence. Chuck noted, "I was afraid of people [as a child]." Jewel replied, "You still are to some extent. . . . You sort of freeze up. . . . Be secure within yourself, and then you can sell yourself when you're able to go back to work."

     Snatches of conversation circled in the air with the smoke. Jewel said, "Even though the doctor who delivered Donna was a little messed up in the head he was a fine man. He was the craziest thing about Donna as anyone I ever saw." Jewel found her visits to Chuck in the mental hospital depressing. "You think it was depressing for *you*," Chuck commented. Chuck talked of a patient who feared he would die in the mental hospital like his father did. Chuck tried to talk with him about it, but the patient did not seem to hear. "Some guys are so far off you can't communicate with them, like mirrors and mirrors in infinite reflections." Chuck went on, "I'm perfectly healthy, but compared with some others I'm still a little off." Jewel encouraged him, "I'm proud you can talk about it, and that makes me feel so good."

8:50 Mrs. Smith jumped up. "Well, this isn't getting my work done, and *you* didn't empty your ashtray. . . ." While washing dishes, she asked how my study of the Smith clan was coming. I told her essentially what I had told Chuck the previous night. She emphasized that the Smith family showed mutual concern and thoughtfulness. For example, Jewel had recently bought Chuck a racer just like the one he had lost as a kid, and Donna had recently bought her mother a peacock feather like the ones the other kids had had when Jewel was a child.

10:00 Jewel was upset about last night. She felt that Chuck ought to tell her where he was going because to do so showed "respect." She held that the Smith family usually told someone when they would be back and where they were going. Cocking her head, she said playfully, "Mean ole' Mother. No wonder you want to go back to the hospital." Chuck told her we would be leaving in a while for the hospital. She said she could get a lot of housework done then. "I'll be here by myself and not have anybody in the way." Chuck said, "You mean I'm in the way—well, thanks a lot." He was joking but he had perceptively picked up the implication of her message.

10:10 Chuck listened for the mail. Mail was a big event in the slow-moving routine of Chuck's days. He looked forward to what he would receive each day. Chuck picked up the mail from the apartment mailbox downstairs.

11:45 Mrs. Smith was working on a crossword puzzle. Chuck helped her by looking up a word in the dictionary.

Afternoon.

12:15 We ate bologna sandwiches for lunch. Then Chuck went back to the couch and read. Chuck felt that he did not need to bathe daily because of his sedentary life, so he did not.

1:15 We left for a lecture to which I had committed myself before this project began. On the way, Chuck spoke of the voices he hears. Currently, he can shift his attention away without obeying them. He had some auditory hallucinations today when he went to get his noon medication. Voices told him not to take the pills, but he did anyway.

During the lecture, Chuck sat listening quietly. At the end I gave him a chance to talk, and he freely told the student nurses at UCLA about his suicide attempt, hospital experience, and depression. He enjoyed the role of knowledgeable resource person, suggesting we should "go on the road" with our "two-man show."

6:20 On our return to the apartment, Chuck told his mother that he had participated in the lecture. Mrs. Smith was somewhat bothered by this, but she resigned herself and somewhat concealed her upset state. The young man expressed his desire to go out to play pool. "Chuck, you'd better watch your pocketbook," Jewel warned.

6:30 Mrs. Smith was cooking supper. Chuck asked, "Did you change the calendar today?" "Yes." "No, you didn't," he said playfully, "*I* did! Caught you in a lie, didn't I?" With a weary smile, "Yeah, you caught me in a big one."

8:00 After picking up Donna at the airport, we returned to her apartment. Mrs. Smith called just as Donna was in the middle of reading a letter from her boyfriend in Germany. "I missed you, too." Donna spoke of being "on a different track" from the two closest men in her life. She felt her interests and values were evolving in different directions from theirs.

8:30 There was normal brother-sister kidding and joking. Chuck told Donna of the fellow at my office who is having a cast of his body made into a coffee table. Donna seemed a bit tired and giddy. Chuck provided her with a psychological explanation of her mood.

8:55 The three of us went bowling. Chuck drank a mixed drink. His bowling scores were in the 120 and 130 range. Each of us won a game.

10:00 We sat in the bar at the bowling alley and talked. Chuck appeared no different from others in the bar. He spoke of his past jobs, of his experience with drugs, and of women in Korea.

12:00 His parents were already asleep and Chuck still had no key to their apartment. We made our beds on Donna's floor and couch and were soon asleep.

February 27, Tuesday

Morning.

6:00 The alarm rang, but Donna went back to sleep. The telephone rang and Chuck answered it. Mr. Smith asked if Donna planned to go to work. She did.

6:30 The telephone rang again and Chuck answered it. (Donna was taking a shower.) Mrs. Smith wanted Donna to call back because it was important. Chuck smoked, put on the coffee water to boil, and went back to bed.

6:35 Donna returned her mother's call. They talked about Donna's job and her excuse for being away from work the past few days.

6:55 Chuck got up.

7:07 We heard a horn blow outside. Chuck called out to Donna that their father had arrived to pick her up.

7:30 We returned to the same pattern of inactivity. But Donna and Jewel agreed that Chuck was awake more now that I was living with him. He also seemed gradually to be confronting his mother more, still on a joking basis, but aggressively. He recognized that because his mother saw a lot of the world in negative-critical terms, she dismissed much of the good out there before allowing herself to explore it. I still perceived some traces of my "honored guest" status, but they were disappearing. At this time Chuck still unlocked and opened my side of the car before he got in on the driver's side, but I put together the ingredients in my own sandwiches, and I rinsed and stacked my own dishes after a meal.

10:45 Chuck and I awakened. Jewel greeted us, "Good morning." I noted, "We slept for an hour and forty-five minutes." "And I've been as busy as a cranberry merchant. . . . " Chuck retorted, "Well, jolly for you." "Yes, jolly for me." Ignoring her, Chuck turned to the car insurance notice he had received in the mail. The ongoing subliminal *contest* seemed to be Jewel's communication: "I'll compare my industriousness with your laziness." Then Chuck's retort: "I'll just stay lazy to show I don't mind being different from you, and I'll get even by exposing your phoniness and my superior intelligence." And Jewel's move: "I'll be careful not to make my middle-class artificiality show, and I won't make many errors in vocabulary, so you can't fault me on that. Anyway, you're sick and not strong-minded. I'll control you." Then Chuck's counter move: "I'll resist your attempts at control by joking or ignoring them." And Jewel's counter to that: "When you do, I'll joke along, but I'll maneuver you with subtlety later." My impression was that when Chuck resorted to sleeping and avoidance to escape his mother's control, he could become suicidal, but that if he *actively* resisted, he might be all right.

11:10 Chuck sat reading on the couch. He did not turn the pages very rapidly. Either he read slowly or he used reading as a front for thinking, for imaginative tripping out, for hallucinating, or simply for avoiding.

11:30 As we ate lunch, Chuck made a sharp verbal comeback. Jewel said, "You sure are feeling better, for a change." A complaint *and a reminder* of when he did not feel so well. Mrs. Smith remarked that she could tell her husband had not been feeling well since their recent trip because he had not been up to his usual wisecracks and mischief. She related the story of years ago when some Negroes in rustling yellow raincoats were being harried by a big dog. The dog was excited by the noise of the coats. "Stand still!" Jewel had called to them. The dog quickly lost interest. "Now you can go!" she had told them. How Jewel enjoyed "helpful" control!

Afternoon.

12:20 Chuck decided to have his eyes examined. He looked up the number of an optometrist and called for an appointment.

12:50 Chuck put down the book and lay on the couch, eyes closed.

1:30 I awoke from unusual dreams of falling, mood swings, and voices. My unconscious was telling me what it thought it was like to go crazy. Mrs. Smith said that she was quite nervous but could see no reason for it. She was trembling, exaggerating this tremor a bit while doing a delicate task. For the most part she was quiet while we slept, but occasionally she would utter moderately loud comments and exclamations. As Chuck went to sleep she said, "Now, don't you go to sleep and let me forget to waken you in time for your appointment.''

1:50 Jewel wakened Chuck for his appointment. While her son was in the bathroom she said to me, "I sure hope he doesn't start sleeping again like he did." She recognized that we had been up late the prior couple of nights, and she saw me sleeping, too. I had become a calibration source for her evaluation of Chuck's sleeping.

3:10 Within an hour we were back again. The telephone rang. It was a family custom to guess who was calling before answering it. It was Donna. Both Jewel and Chuck had guessed correctly.

3:30 Mrs. Smith returned to her dinner preparations. Donna wanted to speak with her. Chuck teased her by pulling the telephone away as Jewel reached for it. She walked away. The second time she approached, however, he gave it to her directly.

5:00 After dinner Mr. Smith turned the television set on to a news program. His wife adjusted it (twice!); she must control even the television.

5:45 Chuck and I helped Donna clean her apartment. Chuck dried the dishes and assisted in making the bed, doing only what Donna asked him to do, nothing more.

6:15 Chuck drank beer at the table and watched Donna continue cleaning. She had a sense of the allowable amount of help she could reasonably expect from her brother and did not trespass beyond that limit. She asked periodically what time it was. Chuck called the hour to her. She asked for our approval of the room's cleanliness and solicited my advice concerning the arrangement of her hair.

6:45 Donna's date arrived. Chuck generated confident conversation with this newly met person.

6:55 Jewel telephoned to tell Chuck that his favorite television show was coming on soon. (I expected we would not return to see it, and we did not.)

7:15 Chuck sat and drank a few beers and listened to rock sounds on the radio. He was half-asleep, half-absorbed in listening.

8:30 Chuck lay on the floor. The radio played meaningless music to an unconscious listener. The cuckoo clock called out the hour and the half hour. The rain drilled into the roof.

11:00 Donna and her date returned and rang the bell, but Chuck, sleeping, did not get up to answer it. Donna used her key and laughed on seeing us lying on the living-room rug. Chuck was dressed, uncovered. Donna turned on the heater and covered him. He wakened for a moment to ask if she had just arrived and was soon asleep again.

February 28, Wednesday

Morning.

8:30 Routine morning: Mrs. Smith prepared breakfast; newspaper reading accompanied by "we'll-see-how-high-my-grocery-bill-will-run-this-week." "I guess David gets mighty sick of hearing all the crap," she said.

8:35 Chuck lay reading a book by Carlos Castaneda.

9:30 Hearing a rattling sound downstairs, Chuck said, "There's the postman." He rose to pick up the mail.

9:35 Chuck was again on the couch. He read and talked with his mother about the phone bill. I continued to struggle against the boredom and meaninglessness of the life that meandered around me.

9:55 Chuck said, "That was good." He had finished the book. Jewel took advantage of the moment. "In a little while, would you go get my *Breeze* (a local newspaper)? You don't have to go right now," she said.

10:25 Chuck and I walked to the mailbox. The exercise felt good. Chuck yawned, "I almost fell asleep on the couch." I told him I felt the same lethargy.

Afternoon.

12:10 Chuck tried to drift off into the nonexistence of sleep, but his mother kept commenting aloud from the paper and managed to keep him awake for a while.

12:30 Just before dropping off to sleep, Chuck quietly counted his money. He was aware that his financial resources were trickling away, and he had no immediate plan for replenishing them.

1:50 Mrs. Smith talked of smells, airsickness, and carsickness. Chuck looked up from his psychology textbook and spoke of getting carsick the first time he came home for a visit from the hospital. Jewel commented that he just sat around the house then, but now he's "doing so well," getting out and around. A pause. . . "This day sure is dragging on," Jewel guessed she had the "lonelies," probably because she had "nothing to do—oh, there are things to do, but. . . "

2:00 Jewel offered us a piece of candy. Chuck took one and left the wrapper on the table. "You good-for-nothing!" she laughed.

3:00 Chuck's mother poured over us a torrent of complaints about impolite store managers, filthy merchandise, and sale items not on the shelves. Such commercial thoughtlessness was not right, I silently agreed, but we sat immersed in her words like utensils in dirty dishwater. Chuck rose from the couch and went to the bathroom. Jewel moved into the kitchen.

March 1, Thursday

Morning.

7:10 Mr. Smith had gone to work. Jewel and Chuck smoked and drank coffee while Jewel ripped into the "resentful," "thieving" employees where she used to work.

7:20 Chuck informed his mother, "I have to go to the hospital today." Jewel decided, "We don't have to go to the hardware store then." Chuck told her it was still all right to go. But Jewel refused. She planned to fix a place for him to study because she could not be quiet in the living room all the time. She did not seem to distinguish between his casual reading and his required reading for school, and he never corrected her.

8:20 Chuck said he attended the outpatient group primarily because it was expected of him and they would worry if he were absent. He got more out of the group led by Dr. Harrison. From the kitchen, while washing dishes, Mrs. Smith talked again of the Christmas party last year, of her wearing an old dress but looking as good as anyone else. Chuck was reminded of a patient who cuts up other jeans to patch his favorite pair. Mrs. Smith spoke of an old prizefighter who "wasn't all there." He lived in a motel they had once managed and usually "went around looking like a tramp." The prizefighter asked for her honest opinion about his clothes one day, and she praised his terrible suit. She knew she was lying but "in his condition that was fine." Her unintended message was that lying to people who "aren't all there" is all right if the lie is intended to make them feel better. The extension to Chuck was obvious.

8:45   The conversation turned to the parents' trip to Europe. With no warning, Jewel exclaimed, "Chuck, your feet smell sour!" Then she returned to her monologue. "Rome is beautiful, but the Romans are the most cold, callous people I've ever seen!"

9:00   Working in the kitchen, Jewel said half to herself, "That was a dangerous thing to do." Chuck looked up from his book, "Did you pull out the plug with wet hands?" "Yes." "Did you take your medicine this morning?" "No." "Mother! You should take your medicine." "If for nothing else, I need you around for that." Mrs. Smith checked to see what Chuck would do if she had a heart attack. She wanted him to call the police first, following her doctor's advice. They talked about heart attacks and fires.

9:30   The postman came. Chuck went down in his bare feet to get the mail.

9:40   The fuse lit by his mother earlier finally produced its fizzle of activity—"Think I'll take a shower."

10:00   Mrs. Smith showed me photos of their trips. She felt Chuck needed to have people around him (although she liked to be alone sometimes—"See how different I am, David?"), and she hoped he would have a job when she and her husband go off on their next trip. Donna would be working all day, and Chuck ought not to be left alone.

10:15   Chuck emerged from the bathroom. Jewel: "Are you going to study now?" Chuck nodded, "Mmm hmm." "I'll try to keep my mouth shut then."

10:25   But her resolve was short-lived. "See, Chuck, Donna loves you very much. She sent you a cute little card." Chuck got up, saying, "I didn't show you what she brought me from there." He took her into the bedroom to show her the fancy bottle cork Donna had bought for him during her ski trip.

10:30   Chuck was back lying on the couch, reading.

11:00 Jewel asked, "What time do you have to leave, Chuck?" "Oh, between 11:30 and 12:00." "I'd better fix lunch. I'd forgotten all about it."

11:15 The telephone rang. "It's Donna," they said in unison. They were right. As usual, Donna handled her mother's controlling tendencies by making demands of her first and then by asking her advice. Thus, she controlled first by asking for control.

11:25 During lunch, Jewel displayed her usual speaking pattern of positive statements followed by critical, gloomy ones. "He's one of the few Italians I like—a nice fellow, not like most young people these days. He's clean. His roommate is a filthy pig. He didn't want to live with a dirty hog." When I heard such speech over a long period, I began to anticipate the pejorative endings, to "wince" psychologically. Also, I became careful, censoring my own actions, worrying about how Jewel would criticize me when I erred.

11:45 On the way to the hospital, Chuck and I talked about the robotized, unthinking, routinized aspect of social existence. He saw it as overwhelmingly negative, but I argued that it provided the predictability that allowed a society to continue to exist.

Afternoon.

1:00 At the group-therapy meeting for outpatients, Chuck questioned a social worker as she might probe another patient. She put him in his place by facetiously calling him "doctor." It felt like a negative, demeaning response to a legitimate query. There was an incongruous mix of "put-downs" by staff along with attempts to make group members contribute. It was a phony, sterile setting. The presenting of artificial images and empty but proper little speeches passed along unnoticed, unchallenged.

3:30 During Dr. Harrison's group, Chuck probed and joked while sitting by the therapist. As usual, at the end of the meeting, Chuck walked the doctor to her car.

4:45 Chuck sat in the office of his former ward and "rapped" with the staff. He described his life as full, busy. He related a few key events (the fishing trip, his visit to his friend's apartment). The implication was that all of his time was accounted for by such events. How unreal was the scroll of life he unrolled for them.

March 2, Friday

Morning.

7:00   When I arrived at the Smiths' apartment, Chuck was still asleep. Jewel was packing Mr. Smith's lunch.

7:10   Jewel filled me in on the hospital visit she and her husband had made to a family friend last night. She talked about his cancer operation, the removal of his ear and nose, and the cutting of a nerve to his shoulder. "Bad, bad, bad!" she exclaimed.

7:20   Mrs. Smith sat for a few minutes over coffee and stared at the wall. She had a habit of suggesting an answer to her own question. When the listener agreed that it was a possible answer, she would bring up new information demolishing that answer. The listener was left with an untenable position. It was like being directed to pick a fruit from a tree only to discover that it was rotten, and that the director had known this all along.

8:00   Chuck was still asleep. Jewel wanted him to go scuba diving with his sister on Sunday. "It would do him a world of good," she said. "It's the kind of group I want him to go out with; it would get rid of some of his insecurity." Donna's scuba diving friends were very close, "almost like a family."

8:10   Mrs. Smith was in the bedroom making the bed. Beds often remained unmade until noon. But today she wanted Chuck to wake up (i.e., she wanted to control his waking) so she puttered (quietly, of course, but with enough disturbance to accomplish her purpose). Finally, she called him. Chuck replied, "Dave here?" She told him that I was. Chuck did not stir. Jewel came out to the kitchen, but she returned to the bedroom to check on Chuck when he did not get up promptly. She opened the front door (unusual behavior for that early in the morning). "It cools the house," she commented. "Seems like the house smells bad this morning." Did a bad smell symbolize interpersonal conflict for her? She said, partly to herself, "I've got a lot to do today. I don't know where to start." She sighed, a bit peeved at Chuck for this intuitive resistance to her beginning a busy day early. She could not prepare breakfast until he got up.

8:30   Mrs. Smith talked of buying chicken from a local take-out place. She decided the people at the stand where she bought it once just did not know how to cook. She expected that when she tried the new place nearby, it would turn out that they did not know how to cook, either. "That much grease'll kill you." Chuck had fallen asleep again.

8:50   Chuck got up and waved to his mother. "Just like a little boy," she remarked. At the table, he dropped a spoon. In the Smith family, any mistake invariably elicited a comment. Jewel jibed, "Butterfingers." "Yes," he replied meekly, still groggy. Jewel jumped in early to tell him what she wanted him to do for her today. "Do you feel like driving me?" "No," he interrupted. "Well, do it anyway . . . if you want to eat." The tone was joking, but the underlying threat-message was apparent.

9:00   Mrs. Smith spoke of the enjoyment involved when the family got together to make ice cream by hand. *But* a piece of ice got in the gear mechanism and tore up the machine. It was broken and unfixable. Again, this speech pattern of light then dark. Chuck lay on the couch with a cup of coffee.

9:30   Chuck went to pick up the mail. Mrs. Smith told me, "I don't open my husband's mail unless it's the Travel Club or the Moving Company Newsletter. Not that he keeps any secrets from me—but that's not the point!" (It was her point to begin with!)

9:35   Jewel reeled off to Chuck a series of recent tragedies involving people at the nursing home she used to manage. "They seem to think that if *I'd* been there, these things wouldn't have happened—but they would."

9:40   Jewel sat in the armchair lost in thought.

10:00   She headed for the bedroom. "I think I'll go lie down for a few minutes. I don't feel too well this morning."

10:30   Donna called. Chuck answered the telephone. He told her we were all sleeping. "We're not lazy; we're tired," he told her in response to her evaluation of the three of us. Jewel emerged from the bedroom to ask if Donna wanted to talk with her.

10:35   Her telephone conversation over, Jewel went downstairs to chat with the apartment manager. Chuck sat on the couch. The rounds of the bookstores he had planned to make today did not materialize.

10:45   Mrs. Smith returned feeling chilled. "People are so rude," she said. She filled us in on the manager's problems with other tenants and the owner of the building. "Boy, I wouldn't manage one of these places again to save my life. . . . Boy, she has got her hands full . . ." Chuck sat stoically, listening and smoking.

10:50   Jewel jumped up to defrost the refrigerator.

11:30   Chuck did not like the book he had been reading. He remarked, "I feel ambivalent this morning." "Well, get with it," Jewel prompted. "Get up and do something!" He retreated into the bedroom to select another book.

11:55   A Spanish-speaking Avon salesgirl, barely fluent in English, came by and sold Chuck some after-shave lotion. He was gentle and helpful to the amateurish and awkward young lady who soon returned to her baby crying in a stroller downstairs. Mrs. Smith stayed unnoticed in the kitchen and bedroom.

Afternoon.

12:15   Jewel reappeared saying she had raised her kids already and shouldn't have to put up with other people's children in this apartment building. Hers were grown, but she didn't do a very good job of raising them, she said. She waited for Chuck to object. He didn't. Jewel pointed out to him that he hadn't spoken up to defend her; then she joked that at least her kids *loved* her or they had her fooled. Again, Chuck made no comment. She asked, "Have you got me fooled?" "Yes," Chuck replied with a straight face. Jewel laughed.

12:55   After lunch, Mrs. Smith rambled while Chuck listened from the couch. Her complaints included drunken neighbors and people who leave in the night without paying their rent. Jewel hated the rug in the apartment. Chuck responded, "It looks perfect to me." His was a subjective-personal perspective (" . . . to me"), and so it was unassailable, unchallengeable, eminently safe.

1:05   Chuck wondered, "Which store do you plan to go to?" (Note that "store" is in singular form.) "I want to go to Thrifty's *first*." (Implying she planned to go to more than one store.)

1:25 Jewel was having difficulty putting her watch on her wrist, but Chuck did not offer to help her. In fact, he almost never offered to help anyone with anything. The closest he came to volunteering for work was when he automatically took out the trash every few days.

1:30 We left for the grocery store. As might be expected, Jewel was backseat-driving. She was pessimistic about the street Chuck turned into, predicting that it was not a through street. She told Chuck, "Go! Go! Go!" when he was slow starting on a green light. In the store, Mrs. Smith commented on the beautiful plants for sale, then (as I winced in anticipation) she said that one of her ferns had died. On leaving, she recommended a different route for getting out of the parking lot only after Chuck was committed to the same one by which we had entered. Her suggested route would have improved our chances of pulling out into traffic.

March 3, Saturday

Morning.

5:50 The alarm rang. Chuck and I got up and dressed. Chuck couldn't find his coat, a small matter that led to a major revelation later the same day.

6:45 We arrived at the sportfishing pier and bought tickets.

7:30 On board the fishing boat, Chuck responded appropriately to aggressive and mistaken criticism by another fisherman. He was taken under the wing of an experienced angler and caught four fish.

Afternoon.

12:30 Our boat returned to the pier. Chuck recalled that last Thursday after school he had left his coat at the Queen of Hearts, a bar with totally nude entertainment. His parents knew nothing of this part of Chuck's life or of his occasionally smoking pot. Donna knew about the latter. Jewel would "disown" him if she knew of the things he had done, he told me. Chuck said the nude entertainment gave him good material for fantasies. He went regularly, about twice a week. As he revealed this hidden side of himself to me, he had the feeling associated with hearing hallucinatory voices, but the voices did not say anything. At the bar he had a few beers, retrieved his coat, and left.

3:05   At home, Chuck showed off his four fish. Mr. and Mrs. Smith praised his catch. Jewel effused, "I'm proud of you, Chuck!" He told them he had found his coat on the floor of the car. Chuck went in to clean the fish.

3:25   Jewel washed out the foul-smelling burlap bag in which we had carried the fish home. She maneuvered Chuck off the couch to help wring it out.

5:10   On the way to a bookstore, Chuck talked of his parents' heavy drinking and the arguments they used to have. He considered their increased age, their worries about health, and their recognition that they had only a few years left in which to appreciate the world to be the key factors in their current total abstinence from alcohol. They did not even permit it in their apartment. The family's joking together was also a recent phenomenon, according to Chuck, having begun within the past couple of years.

8:15   We went to the Queen of Hearts again. Chuck paid over $5 for drinks and tips as he watched the show. He had superficial joking relations with the waitress/dancers. His favorite dancer had light auburn hair and creamy, smooth skin. His eyes fixed on the sinuous movement. Chuck wondered mischievously what I would dream about that night. He mused of his impotence in Korea at times when he was under the influence of alcohol and the disappointment this created for the women there. Impotence was also a problem for him when he was taking a certain tranquilizer.

10:30   When Chuck left the bar, I asked to drive back because of his drinking. In the car, Chuck talked about the voices he heard. I asked if they ever occurred when he was driving. He said they tell him such things as "Don't change lanes." I told him of a voice I had heard from the back seat when he was driving. "Go! Go! Go!" the voice had said.

We returned to his parents' apartment. Mr. Smith had gone to work. Chuck informed his mother only of our going to the bookstore and picking up my mail. Jewel told him accusingly to use some Listerine and get the smell of booze off his breath. We ate dessert while she watched television. Chuck's money had dwindled to about $150.

March 4, Sunday

Morning.

7:15   I asked Chuck what sorts of stresses he had experienced since coming home. He replied that not catching a fish right away was stressful. I asked what positive experiences he had experienced. He offered the following: movies, bowling, fishing, book-hunting, having his eyes examined, and getting his car fixed. What did he look forward to? Getting his G.I. Bill check, getting his glasses, completing the paper due in his psychology class. So far, he had not wished to be back in the hospital. "Wonder how long I'll be out before I go back in again." Chuck said he did not feel like going back at that time, "but you never can tell." I asked if he could offer advice to other newly discharged patients. "Tell them to keep busy most of the day, to keep their minds off their problems and not dwell on them." Jewel would have said the same.

7:45   Chuck showed Jewel a print he bought last night. Her response: "Now that leaves me completely void. I like the colors, but . . . " If Mrs. Smith were rich like Howard Hughes, she would restore the Sistine Chapel and stand right there and supervise to see that they did the job right. Jewel wondered whether her son planned to go back to school in summer. He did. She asked if there were a break between quarters and for how long. She inquired whether Chuck would like to see his aunt. Again, she got an affirmative answer. "But it's impossible now." She dropped the subject. She was keeping secret the proposed trip for Chuck, planning to surprise him later.

8:10   Jewel thought the apartment was dark and depressing. She wanted something more cheerful and asked Chuck to help hang some plants out on the balcony. Chuck looked at her, smiling. "What do you want me to do—fall off and kill myself?"

    Chuck mentioned a dream from last night. Intending to

put on a conservative tape for a "vague" audience, he instead put on a tape of the rock musical *Hair*. He was upset, but he did not notice the audience's reaction. The symbolism seemed obvious. By taking me to his nude bar, he had revealed a more radical side of himself than he had intended. My reaction was, as usual, noncommittal.

8:25 Between bites of cereal, Mrs. Smith said, "This place won't do; it's too small. If you'll behave yourself and stay home (i.e., stay out of the hospital), we can move." Chuck warned her, "I'd wait a while before I moved." Jewel had heard him. "We depended on you too many times before. We'll wait." Chuck impishly threatened, "I'll probably go berserk some morning, scream, break things." Jewel countered, "You're not *that* deranged. If you did, Dad wouldn't let you come back. I'd probably have a heart attack and it'd kill me." Cards on the table. Who held the trumps?

11:55 Chuck woke up. "Every night I have dreams of the theater or of the military, sometimes both." As he dozed this morning, Chuck had a dream of a character in a play, a beggar, who the audience thought was Mary Poppins. But when she took off her makeup, she turned out to be not Mary Poppins but a beautiful woman. Then he told me of a beautiful girl he had met through his ex-fiancee. He saw the girl on television once playing the part of a frog. It was hard to discern how much was the contribution of his imagination to what he actually saw and how much to his attempt to spice up the story in the telling.

12:00 Chuck got up and made coffee. He heard a voice call "Hey!"

Afternoon.

2:50 Chuck sat on the couch, reading. Mrs. Smith worked on a crossword puzzle. Mr. Smith sat at the table smoking (he had quit recently), listening to the radio. Jewel, too, had tried to cut down, but she continued smoking throughout my stay there. "Guess no one can get this radio to work but me. Radios are like wives—you've got to humor 'em," Mr. Smith remarked. Later, he made a slip of the tongue and his wife gleefully shouted, "I got you! Got you!" Chuck, too, joined in the heckling, which was taken good-naturedly. They seemed overreacting to the mistake, but it fit the pattern in which Jewel initiated playful aggressiveness and her husband enjoyed sniping back at her.

3:25 Jewel told Chuck to move over. He did not. She sat on him. After a while he erupted, "Cut it out!" "Move over." He did.

She called Donna. "What did you do today?" Chuck asked if he could come over and listen to tapes. Donna replied, "If you'll be a good boy." Jewel laughed. Chuck agreed to be good.

5:00 Back at the parents' apartment, there was joking and family chatter while Jewel prepared dinner. Mr. and Mrs. Smith exchanged verbal blows. Mrs. Smith, laughing, retorted with, "You do and you'll need a new nose!" And later, "When are you going to grow up?" Again, she laughed.

6:15 After supper, Donna wanted to know, "You guys going to come over for a while?" Chuck offered, "We'll take you to the laundromat." But somewhere along the line, Donna had decided not to do her laundry that night after all.

7:05 Donna suggested we leave soon for a movie. On the way, Donna and I talked while Chuck was the quiet but attentive driver. Donna directed her questions and comments at me. I told her of my purposeful passivity and spoke generally of the patterns of interaction and activity levels that would emerge from the recorded notes of individual acts.

10:35 After the movie, we returned to Donna's apartment. She invited us up for a while. She spoke of her live-fully-for-the-moment philosophy. Chuck had another beer.

10:55 Donna asked if we were going to stay all night (a legitimate question but also a hint for us to leave). Chuck said we'd go.

11:00 We left, after receiving hugs from Donna, and soon arrived at the other apartment. Having borrowed his mother's key, Chuck let us in. His parents were asleep.

March 5, Monday

Morning.

6:30 Mrs. Smith was up already, fixing lunch. She was not in a joking mood and called her husband a "smart aleck." "You're talking like a dopey this morning." Clearly, she maintained a no-nonsense attitude. Mr. Smith dryly re-marked, "I just won't associate with you." Jewel seemed happy about that. Chuck was still asleep.

6:45 There was a considerable difference between the amount of disturbance in the bedroom when his father was asleep there and when the sleeper was Chuck. That morning, Mrs. Smith was in the bedroom making the bed, hanging up clothes, and generally rattling around. But when Charles, Sr., was asleep, she would stay out, fuss over keeping the door closed and keeping the curtains drawn. She apparently wanted Chuck to get up. So, as usual in this sort of contest, he would probably resist by feigning sleep until she made a direct call to him.

6:50 "I think when we go to the laundry I'm going to let this house air out real good. Get rid of this cigarette smell." "When my husband goes to work, I'll fix you and Chuck some breakfast." She said Chuck would be getting up soon (!). She planned to do her laundry that morning and have Chuck take Donna to the laundry that night. Her goal was to "keep him busy. When he's preoccupied [sic] he doesn't have time to think." She seemed to have forgotten his plans to go to the library that day.

7:12 Chuck got up. "Good morning, everybody." He started right in teasing Jewel, "putting her on" with an imaginary tale. Jewel laughed. "One good thing about it, I caught on before you started laughing at me." She told him we were going to do the laundry today. Chuck told us that he dreamed the night before of a high school with a high fence all around it. He was outside the fence, and girls inside were kicking around a tennis ball. Once a ball came over the fence and he threw it back. Then he was swinging. A fat girl walked in front of his swing so he spread his legs, caught her, and continued swinging with her. Jewel changed the subject. "I hate for Daddy to go to the grocery store with me. It doesn't matter how much a thing is, he says to go ahead and get it. He just plays into their hands."

7:28 "Here comes the earthquake again." The sound was of a door closing and the stairs rumbling as a man ran down them. Jewel grumbled "And he doesn't even know that he's doing it."

7:40 Newspaper in hand, Chuck informed us, "I started to read this and a voice said, 'Don't read it.' " He laughed and looked to his upper right playfully and asked, "Why? Why? Why?"

7:45 Mrs. Smith called us to breakfast. As usual, Chuck delayed. "Better eat it while it's warm." She waited. Finally she called him sharply. He got up from the couch and came to the table. Mrs. Smith pressed on. "After breakfast you can start putting the laundry in the car." He parried by telling her that he had to go to the hospital today. She asked if he wanted to do the laundry the next day. He said he did not, but that he would go to the hospital and library after we did the laundry today. Both jockeyed for control.

I noticed that sometimes it appeared as if "please" or "thank you" was said in order to avoid criticism or attack for being impolite rather than as an expression of pleasure or gratitude.

Jewel believed that having his own car gave Chuck a sense of independence. She considered the car very important to his adjustment. In the past, even when the parents did not feel like taking him to places he needed to go, they did anyway. She knew that Chuck sensed his being picked up and dropped off by his parents was a strain on them. She said all this aloud in Chuck's presence. "Am I right, Chuck?" He agreed, "Unhunh," and seemed uninterested. She said, "Now I'm depending on him a little bit, so I'm paying him back." "You old meany," Chuck kidded her. "I just hope and pray you can get some income just to get you through school." "I'll get the G.I. Bill." "Yes, but you know how *that* is. You were so depressed about that one time." Jewel went on, "When a mental patient comes out of the hospital, he isn't ready to go to work. His parents know that and he does, too. It must be depressing to ask his parents for money for gas, school books, and things like that. He's draining the heck out of his parents and some of them just can't afford it." She believed this would cause embarrassment, then depression, and he would have to go back to the hospital. She felt that there should be some sort of fund for ex-patients in situations like that. A person needs entertainment but has no money for it.

8:50   We went to the laundromat. After carrying in the clothes, Chuck sat down with a coke and a copy of *Rosemary's Baby*. Mrs. Smith filled six laundry tubs, added soap, and went about the business of washing clothes.

9:45   Jewel called Chuck. He knew before asking, but responded, "What do you want?" "Two hands." He got up and helped her fold clothes. She dropped one corner of the sheet and said, "What's wrong with me?" Criticizing herself with the same vehemence she criticized others.

10:00   We returned to the apartment. Mrs. Smith thanked us for helping. Chuck took the mailbox key and checked for mail, but there was none. Mrs. Smith offered to pack a lunch for us. She asked, "You know why I'm anxious to get rid of you boys?" Chuck jumped in, "Your boyfriend is coming over." "Chuck, even that is vulgar." No, she didn't want us "underfoot" while she cleaned the house. She suspected that when she finished she would be ready for bed. She was tired because she had been awakened by Mr. Smith, who had made a loud noise pouring cereal in a bowl in the morning. "He doesn't realize it, but . . . " Again, Jewel was upset that her world was full of people who did thoughtless things without awareness. She "rattled" verbally. It seemed to be a way of dissipating mild tension, of keeping others' attention on her, and perhaps of focusing her own thoughts.

10:20   Jewel ate, making Chuck wait for her to pack lunches. Chuck reminded her that we were going to the V.A.

10:30   Chuck reminded his mother again of the sack lunches. Still she sat and talked. Jewel asked me to give the research checks to her husband and not to her in the future (actually, I gave the check to Chuck who, in turn, gave it to her). "He's the man of the house," she said. She knew "it sounds passé, but he's the breadwinner."

10:38   She got up to fix the lunches. "Are you about ready to go? I didn't want to fix them before you were ready." Chuck sat waiting on the couch.

11:10   We arrived at the hospital. As we walked toward the canteen, Chuck heard a voice call him "knucklehead." It was a calm, sexless voice.

Afternoon.

2:40 At the Queen of Hearts, Chuck drank five beers. As he watched the topless-bottomless dancers, he commented, "This sure beats looking at those hospital walls." He sometimes speculated on what the dancers were doing during the day. They were objects of daydreams as well as of nightly fantasies. I asked what he thought the waitresses thought of him. "I don't think about that." He supposed they did not *all* like him. Some knew his name, some saw him just as another customer. My impression was that they liked his money, nothing more. Their banter was casual, almost impersonal. Chuck said his first breakdown came after drinking a six-pack per night alone in his apartment following work at a hamburger stand run by a bitchy female. Something snapped, and the change frightened him to the point of panic. Now he felt safer in that he knew he could always return to the hospital if he started going downhill again.

5:20 After dinner at the apartment, Mr. Smith sat reading the paper. He was indignant about the gasoline-rationing proposal. "Impeach them!" he insisted.

5:40 When Donna called, Mrs. Smith asked her daughter to join her for shopping. She invited Chuck also, but Chuck, lying in the bedroom, wanted more sleep. He told her that maybe we would go over to Donna's later.

6:55 I awakened Chuck to find out if he was going to get up any more that night. If not, I planned to go home. He decided to get up.

7:00 Chuck, sitting comfortably in the armchair, commented on the voices we could hear from the next apartment. They were a result of the combination of loud voices and thin walls, his father suggested.

7:20 Jewel and Donna returned from marketing. Donna began showing us photos from her last two trips. Jewel got mad at the neighbors who had just tapped on the wall for us to be more quiet. Mr. Smith exaggerated his agreement with Jewel's comments to the point of absurdity. She was half-irritated and snipped at him. He retorted, "Don't get 'horsey' with me." Mr. Smith kept his wife's criticisms focused on precise issues and details. He did not allow her anger and gloom to spill over onto broad areas.

7:55   Chuck and Jewel had a playful swatting fight.

8:02   Mrs. Smith got up to take her medicine, mentioning her purpose. "Hey, Mom," said Chuck, playfully. "Why don't you take your medicine?"

8:12   Mrs. Smith prompted, "Donna wants to go home, Chuck." Donna interrupted, "No, let him watch the show." "I don't care about the show." Chuck pulled himself out of the chair.

8:20   After arriving at Donna's apartment, Chuck and I talked while Donna was on the telephone with a boyfriend. Chuck said that sometimes he forgets his medication. Most often he forgets at noontime (this week he forgot or did not have the pills with him for two days).

   In Chuck's suicide attempt, his companion talked Chuck out of shooting himself in the head, saying he might not die and would live on as a vegetable. After the attempt, Chuck had dreams in which he relived the experience right up to the shooting and would awaken yelling "No!"

   Chuck went to the liquor store; he brought back beer and soft drinks.

9:50   Donna began throwing pillows at us. Chuck asked if we ought to go home. "I couldn't give a bigger hint," Donna replied.

March 6, Tuesday

Morning.

7:00   Jewel got up and worked on her husband's lunch. Mr. and Mrs. Smith really enjoyed their joking, aggressive banter; they started right out with it in the morning. Mr. Smith's deflating dry wit kept Jewel entertained. She called him a little boy and told him to cut it out, but she encouraged the exchanges by her criticism and controlling behavior.

7:40   Chuck got up when Jewel went into the bedroom. "I'm sorry, Chuck, did I wake you up?" Chuck helped himself to a cup of coffee and told her, "You're mean." "That's the reason you love me."

Chuck made an uncustomary request, "Want to hand me that ashtray?" "No." "You better." An interesting role reversal. "What do you have to do today besides study, Chuck?" she asked. "Nothing. I don't have to study today." "You don't?" "It's only Tuesday, isn't it?" In that case, Jewel wanted to go to the hardware store.

8:05 Chuck reminded her to take her medicine. Jewel jumped up, "Oh thank you, Chuck." She hated to be "tied down" to taking medication at a specific time or to any routine or schedule.

8:10 As we sat down to breakfast, I told Chuck we needed a knife for the jelly. He slipped behind me and playfully put an arm around my neck and a butter knife to my throat. I passed it off quickly, automatically trusting him, but afterward I thought about the gesture. Was he telling me not to try to control him as his mother did? I decided to worry only if the playful threat was repeated.

8:55 Jewel finished cleaning the kitchen. She made a production of how hard it was and how good it felt to have it done. "You'd think it never gets cleaned the way I carry on." Chuck was lying on the couch, as usual. She wanted him to help with the task of drilling a hole for hanging potted ferns.

9:00 Mrs. Smith told a story of kindness about a plant gift from a lady she had never seen. She wished she did not like plants so much because she had no place to put them.

9:25 She finished dusting, plopped in her chair and said, "Hooray and hallelujah!"

9:35 The mailman made his usual morning noises. I thought no one else had noticed. Jewel stirred from her chair. "Think I need to go back to bed. Getting restless now; nothing to do." Chuck was lying down, reading.

9:45 He got up, saying, "I heard the mailman come by," and went out to get the mail.

Jewel talked of the faults of rich people, racial problems, and marriage breakups. I commented that I thought she was very sensitive to the sad and negative side of life. She agreed but did not see this as one-sided or unbalanced, perceiving an equal interest in positive aspects.

Afternoon.

1:00 We returned to the apartment. Mrs. Smith couldn't find her
      key. Chuck volunteered to get the manager's key. He re-
      turned and let us into the apartment. Jewel emptied her
      purse on the floor but still could find no key. She called the
      restaurant and the hardware store we had just visited. I asked
      why Chuck did not have a key. Jewel considered it unneces-
      sary for him to have one since he could borrow hers when-
      ever he needed it. Anyway, the manager issued only two
      keys, one for her and one for her husband. Chuck offered to
      take his father's key and have another made for her. Jewel
      told him he might as well have two made, one for himself
      also, and she would pay for them.

1:40 After a couple of initial hints, Mrs. Smith prodded, "Well, do
      you want me to go get the drill?" Chuck nodded. She went
      off humming into the bedroom.

1:45 Mother and son drilled and hung her potted plants. Jewel
      supervised, but Chuck held firm when they disagreed and
      won his points. She whispered to me that she knew "this is a
      lot of bother, but it sure beats him sitting around."

2:10 Chuck finished and sat in the chair, grinning, "Well, now I
      have to rest for about four hours." His mother laughed.

2:30 Mrs. Smith was working. Chuck was sitting. Jewel talked
      about seeing several young girls smoking what she suspected
      to be marijuana. She said their parents probably knew noth-
      ing about it. Chuck looked at me knowingly. He coolly
      mentioned that Donna had smelled marijuana at a rock
      concert she attended.

3:00 "The people I feel sorry for are those that can't occupy their
      minds or find themselves something to do." Jewel embedded
      this statement in a larger conversation. Chuck invited her to
      go with him to a nearby shopping center. She declined.
      "Maybe tomorrow. Do you have to go today?" "Yes. I've got
      to study tomorrow."
          Instead of shopping, however, we went to the Queen of
      Hearts bar. We sat through two complete cycles of the three-
      girl show, as usual. Chuck drank six or seven beers. He asked
      if I sometimes felt as if I were cheating and living on bor-

rowed time. I told him no, but that I felt obligated to live productively. I asked if recently he had been coming to the bar more often than usual. He said that he was coming more often because the newness of being home was beginning to wear off. I asked if the bar would become less interesting, too. He thought so, eventually. After two and a half hours, his speech was slightly silly. Fantasies and reveries were taking over as he stared into space or at the dancers.

5:00 As he drove home, Chuck said the world seemed unreal. His driving, however, seemed only minimally impaired. Jewel asked me if Chuck got what he wanted (referring to the books we had supposedly gone to buy). I told her I was not sure what he was looking for, but I did not think he got it. I told her to ask him directly.

6:00 After dinner, Chuck called Donna and told her we would come over in a while to take her to do the laundry.

7:00 On the way to the laundromat, Donna made two suggestions: one concerned the best route to take and one involved where to park. Chuck resisted her efforts to control; in both cases he did what he preferred to do.

7:35 Chuck remarked, "My head feels sleepy, but my body wants to do something." But he would not sleep in a public place. Donna playfully sprayed water in my face, and ran off saying, "I've got to go check on my clothes."

9:40 We returned to Donna's apartment after shopping at various stores. Chuck drank beer and smoked. Donna told him of a job opening, but he felt it was unsuitable.

10:15 Chuck decided we should leave before we got locked out of his parents' apartment. Looking back over today, I recalled that both Donna and Jewel independently asked if I would maintain contact with the family after my research was over. I could see a milder form of Mrs. Smith's controlling efforts exhibited by Donna, but it was more tempered, subtler. The brother-sister interaction was mutually satisfying and reciprocally considerate. I could not say what the family was like in the past, but the closeness was genuine at this time even when exaggerated somewhat by Jewel.

I recalled that Chuck revealed at the bar that he used to be very religious and wanted to save the world, but he discovered that people were going to do what they wanted to do anyway, so he had given up those ideals. And now, he told me, he was interested in satanism.

March 7, Wednesday

Morning.

7:40   Chuck sat on the couch, drank coffee, and smoked.

7:45   Chuck planned to duplicate the remaining key, but he realized that unless they found his mother's key, he would have to wait until his father got home with his key.

7:50   Jewel queried, "Chuck, are you nervous this morning?" "Not especially. Why?" "I can usually tell," she said, "You sit in the same place and crack your knuckles one after the other." She tried to get him to study in the bedroom today, but he resisted, giving no reason.

7:55   Jewel got up to get dressed and soon emerged wearing the black sweater and slacks outfit that she called her "witch's costume."

8:10   "You don't need to go back to sleep, Chuck. Breakfast will be ready in a few minutes."

9:40   While Chuck was downstairs mailing a letter, Mrs. Smith asked me if he had been drinking yesterday. "You're putting me in a bind," I replied. She said *her* mental state was as important as *Chuck's*. I told her that was why she should ask Chuck directly. She said she would.

9:45   Chuck was lying on the couch rereading his class notes.

10:00 Chuck rolled to a sitting position, "I think I'll take a shower."

        Mrs. Smith reminded him twice to rinse out the tub. She repeated that she always cleaned it after she took a bath. After Chuck went in to shower, Jewel wanted to talk to me about his previous hospital admission. She made certain I understood, "It's not anything his father or I did." His parents took Chuck to San Diego and spent a lot of money (he paid his own way), but the effects on his mood wore off in a few days. Then he would get up for meals only. She expected him to start this pattern again because she detected beer on his breath recently. This expectation is presently incongruent with reality; Chuck has been relatively active in spite of his drinking. "I know more about this than you or anyone else," she emphasized. She assured me that she would not tell him not to drink, but he had promised not to drink and drive. Whenever he left the house, she told him to drive carefully. If he ever had a few beers and got into an accident, the police would be hard on him. Instead of nagging, she explained that she drops hints. She offers suggestions about his not drinking and encourages him to work, not just to be an "educated fool." She said she loved him as a son and as a human being. Her husband told her, "Jewel, you can't afford to ruin your health over someone who won't listen." She believed Chuck's depression had contributed to her heart trouble. She protected Chuck on the job. When Chuck was hired at the nursing home where she worked, she told the boss, "Don't say one word to him. Jump on *me*; I can take it." "I was so proud of Chuck," she went on. There was a pause as she reviewed what she had just said. "I still am because I love him," she continued. "Some of the books he reads aren't good for him. But it'd be foolish to tell him not to read them." "He's in his early thirties, after all," I reminded her. She felt Chuck was better this time than ever on his return from the hospital. In what ways, I wondered. "He's more jovial, more affectionate to Donna and me, and even to his Dad." Chuck was still somewhat rebellious, she felt, but his attitude was better, even though sometimes he rejected her ideas and efforts.

10:35 Chuck emerged from the shower. He sat on the couch and smoked. Mrs. Smith called herself an impatient old woman, already looking for the yarn she had sent away for not long ago. She said she didn't know who to contact to straighten out a problem involving a mail order company. "I thought you knew everything," Chuck jabbed. She laughed. I was struck by Chuck's flat, impassive style when he is around Jewel and by her liveliness when she is around him. These are mutually reinforcing facades that drop or fade in other settings with other persons.

10:45 Mrs. Smith offered, "Does anyone want anything from the deli?" Chuck wanted a cola. "Got any money?" He did.

11:20 Donna called and talked with Chuck. He sounded genuinely interested and pleased to talk with her. His voice became animated. After he had hung up, with disappointment in her voice Mrs. Smith asked, "You mean she didn't want to talk to her mother?" "She said she'd talk to you before she left work."

11:35 Chuck looked up. "What are we going to have for lunch?" Jewel responded disinterestedly, "I don't know." "Do we have any roast beef left?" "Mmm hmm." She continued to pursue her Wednesday newspaper ads. In this setting, as in board-and-care facilities, the schedule and the convenience of those in power determined to some degree when meals would be served. But Chuck had the options, not available in board-and-care facilities, to cook his own food, eat with the family, or wait and eat after the others finished.

11:45 Chuck was still lying and reading on the couch. I opened the door because the room was hot and smoke-filled.

11:55 Jewel stirred. "Aren't you beginning to get a little cool, David?" I took the hint and shut the door. She got up and emptied ashtrays. Was this a pattern of hers—control of others followed by service?

Afternoon.

12:05 At last Mrs. Smith announced lunch, "Now it's ready." Chuck was hungry and responded quickly. After sandwiches and ice cream, we cleared off our dishes.

2:25 Mrs. Smith talked of her nimbleness and how young she looks in comparison with Barbara Stanwyck and Julie Ackermann. The latter looked "even uglier than I am." Chuck took advantage of the opening, "That's pretty ugly." She laughed, got up, and went over and hugged him. "You don't mean that. You love your mama." Chuck continued lying on the couch. A few minutes later she laughed and said, "I'll get you." Chuck didn't know what she was talking about and asked, "What?" She explained she would get him for saying that. "I was only kidding." Mrs. Smith said, "I know. . . . I don't know why I have tears in my eyes every time I laugh. . . . Daddy says I have to be different. I cry when I'm happy."

2:35 Chuck appeared to be going back to sleep.

2:50 Chuck was dozing on the couch. Mrs. Smith called from the bedroom and held up a huge pair of scissors. She said, "David, this is one of my scissors. I've got every size and shape in the books." She had proudly displayed her scissors collection before.

2:55 Mrs. Smith sorted noisily through a button collection while seated in her chair. Chuck dozed. She puttered and shifted around and talked to herself and to me. She appeared to be trying to keep Chuck awake. A few minutes later she dropped her needle and got tickled at the idea of what Charles, Sr., would say if he sat on it.

3:00 Mrs. Smith looked concerned. "Do you feel bad, Chuck?" Without moving, he grunted "No." I might have responded to such pressing inquiry with anger—"Get off my back!" but Chuck quietly accepted her solicitous queries.

3:15 Awakened by his mother's voice, Chuck shifted into action, heading for the bathroom to trim his moustache. "You fellows have been regular gadabouts this week. If you haven't been on the go for me, you've been on the go for your-selves." "Yeah," Chuck replied and was gone.

3:20 Chuck said he was going to Donna's to pick up the painting outfit they planned to send to Mrs. Smith's sister. I gave him my key to Donna's apartment.

3:30 Mrs. Smith wanted to talk more. A television program the night before dealt with a family that facilitated their son's suicidal behavior. Perhaps the program caused Mr. and Mrs. Smith to confront the possibility that they contributed to Chuck's problems. Mrs. Smith showed a great deal of defen-siveness the next day. She and Mr. Smith had talked about Chuck's suicidal tendencies and had decided he would prob-ably try again. She did not know how it would hit her when he did. She was trying to be careful not to say anything that would be interpreted by Chuck to mean she felt he was a burden. She cited a couple of things that she had said and then, thinking over the ways he could misinterpret them, had added phrases or sentences so that he would not feel bad. I suggested that her being too careful might not be necessary, that Chuck knew she cared about him, and he knew she would not intend to hurt him. After all, Chuck was an adult and did not need to be overprotected.

Mrs. Smith spoke of how she had made a thriving success

of a hamburger stand by making each customer feel he was the most important person on earth. I wonder if this sales-orientation, resulting in artificial self-presentation and over-played interest in others, might not be a strong influence on interactions in our society and, more specifically, in this family. She *tried hard* to make Chuck feel like he was paying them back for all they had done, that he was useful, that he was loved. But it was so obvious she was *trying* to do this.

She felt, as I did, that Chuck wanted to get away for a while. That was why he chose to go to Donna's just when I was planning to shower. She had observed in the past that when Chuck smoked as he did this day, forcefully exhaling the smoke, there was something bothering him. That was why she asked earlier if he felt bad. But she had learned not to probe any deeper than she did. Chuck did not open up to her probing. So she would worry now until he came home. I thought that he knew she would worry.

4:45   Chuck walked in.

5:00   Chuck sat rocking in the chair and smoking.

5:05   Chuck called a hardware shop to find out about their key duplicating service. Mrs. Smith said she would give him money to pay for *her* key (earlier she had said she would pay for both).

5:15   We left on several errands. I asked Chuck if anything were bothering him. His mother was worried. He said that nothing was bothering him. I let him know I would believe him.

When parking at the hardware shop, Chuck almost backed into a car that was entering the lot. I shouted "Whoa!" and we missed the other car. I simply could not be passive in such a situation. As we exited from the car, the other driver apologized. Surprising, since the near accident was clearly Chuck's fault. He had two duplicate keys made.

5:30   Chuck tried the keys in the apartment door. They worked properly.

5:40   Chuck sat in the chair, smoking.

5:50   Mr. Smith showed Chuck the peeling skin on his hands. After a few seconds, Chuck, uninterested, started watching television while Mr. Smith continued to explain to him the symptoms and possible causes. Mr. Smith hinted that he would like some tea. Jewel jumped up to prepare it, exaggerating her response to the hint. Then she noticed that the television was too loud and had her husband get up to lower the volume. While up, Mr. Smith changed the television channel. His authority in channel selection was unquestioned. Punch and punch and counterpunch.

March 8, Thursday

Morning.

7:20 Chuck got up. He seemed in a good mood as he sat talking about school. Jewel took over the conversation, describing the travel films that she had seen the night before.

7:35 Jewel moved into the kitchen, still talking. Chuck seemed exceptionally alert. In school last night, the instructor had lectured on phantom limbs. Jewel knew a fellow whose leg was cut off. "He had a very strong mind or he'd have gone off the deep end."

7:45 Chuck was lying on the couch, moving his feet and toes while conversing. The discussion shifted to clairvoyance. Mrs. Smith said she "knew of" her husband's auto accident a couple of hours before being informed by telephone. Chuck had been wrong about the cause of his father's arm disfigurement. It was not a result of the auto accident but of a fall from a porch during his childhood. Mr. Smith had thought about having it rebroken and repaired, but Jewel had dissuaded him, fearing complications. She remarked, "I never notice it." These were almost exactly Chuck's words when we had talked about the arm earlier.

Chuck animatedly showed me some of his art prints. His mood continued elevated. As he went into the bedroom to put away the prints, Jewel winked at me, smiled, and made an "okay" sign with her fingers.

8:25 Chuck commented, "There are so many singing groups out now." Mrs. Smith came in, "And they can't sing."

9:05 Chuck was lying on the couch studying algebra for his electricity course. "I'd go crazy trying to figure this out," he groaned.

9:15 Chuck asked me to help him with the algebra. We worked on it for an hour.

10:40   Chuck mused, "David, what do you call it when you can't retain something?" Jewel leaped, "Stupidity!" She laughed.

11:15   "David, you might think I'm crazy to go to such trouble to send these hobby kits to Daisy (Jewel's sister). We want to keep her occupied. When I was down there she said, 'Jewel, did you ever think of committing suicide?' I just about went into shock." Mrs. Smith told her she had thought of suicide "so she wouldn't feel all by herself; but it was a lie. That's the reason Donna and I are going all out of our way to give her something to do—to get her mind off of herself." Chuck, of course, heard his mother tell me this tale.

11:20   Chuck hinted that it was getting late. Jewel jumped up to fix lunch.

11:25   From the couch, "I don't want any bouillon." "How did you know, Chuck?" "I just had a feeling." Perhaps he heard the boiling water.

11:30   We ate lunch. Mrs. Smith lectured us about every family member being a spoke in the wheel; all are useful and important. She said her drooping last week was mental, a response to her husband's flu. She kidded Chuck that sometimes she didn't know if he were worth all the trouble he made. She asked if he thought he was, and he said, "No." She interpreted his response as kidding, too.

11:40   Chuck was seated working on his algebra.

11:45   Mrs. Smith wanted to put a lamp on the desk and have Chuck study there. I mentioned that Chuck seemed satisfied with the arrangements as they were. Mrs. Smith said, "Yes, but every little bit helps." She needed to control even his study area.

11:55   Chuck emptied the trash.

Afternoon.

12:25   We arrived at the hospital. Chuck decided to go to the canteen despite threatening clouds. He told me he had been feeling nervous for the past few days. He felt especially tense that day. His pace slowed, perhaps because he was early, or perhaps because the hospital grounds provided a situation cue that slowed his pace.

12:50   Chuck played pool with me and won, as usual. He greeted several patients and staff members and carried on small talk.

1:00   Chuck sat down and waited for group therapy to begin. He had been depressed the night before, thinking of quitting school when he knew he would be faced with the difficult algebra problems. If he dropped one of the two courses he would no longer be eligible for the G.I. Bill. Therefore, he decided that if he quit one, he would quit school altogether. . . .

1:05   The group meeting began. Several members were absent because of the rain. Chuck was not paying much attention. He was looking out the window. When he was called on to share his school experiences, he spoke truthfully about the time he spent studying, his difficulty with algebra, and the lowering of his mood when he encountered difficulty. He told his physician that the medication was wearing off. In response to the social worker's query about what he did during the day, he said, "We[!] read and nap and read and nap."

       Chuck told me he did not drink much the night before because he did not feel like it and because he was afraid of what he might do since he was so depressed. The bottomless dancing was to be banned by law the next day, Chuck was anticipating trouble with the algebra on the next morning, and he was upset by my not going to the bar with him any more. After the group meeting, Dr. Raphael added Thorazine and Elavil to Chuck's Artane and Stelazine. This was a characteristically *medical* response to disorders. In Chuck's therapy groups, too, the "illness" interpretation of mental disorder was stressed.

4:50   We went to his former ward for coffee. Barbara Bristol asked Chuck about his recent nervousness. Did he mean he was tense or hallucinating? He said he was hallucinating. She asked him why. He gave what was elsewhere an acceptable reason—the algebra in his electricity course. She wanted to know if that were enough to make him hallucinate? He guessed so. She thought his electricity study was supposed to be a "fun" course, that is, the easier of the two. She asked him what was depressing him. He said he did not know. He said he had seen faces coming out of the walls, but had some control over these visual illusions. Two hours earlier he had taken one Thorazine, and about one hour after taking it he had felt calm. Last night he had seen a nude dancer turn into a white egg with rat's legs. Chuck said he woke up four or five times per night, dreamed of nude women a lot, had some trouble getting his bearings on awakening, and then went back to sleep.

He gave a pretty straight account of his daily activities to the social worker, not embellishing much except his speed at reading. He told Barbara that the movie, *Up the Sandbox*, was terrible. After the movie, he had described it as "so-so" to me.

Barbara told Chuck that depression is an attitude. Since we can *choose* our attitudes, Chuck must enjoy his depression. He gave a noncommittal response to this line of reasoning. Barbara suggested that Chuck read *Man's Search for Meaning*. She also recommended that he get more exercise so he would sleep better. Further, she recommended he visit on her ward more and attend the recreation group there. He appeared to consider what she said but did not commit himself. Barbara said she could "feel" Chuck's depression; it brought her mood down a bit just by talking with him. When she asked me if I felt low, I replied that I did not feel any lower than yesterday. "He's always depressed anyway," Chuck quipped. I let his comment pass for the moment but explained later to Chuck that although I am quiet, I do not feel depressed. Barbara was puzzled that Chuck did not visit the ward more often. She was interested in helping Chuck arrange a living situation away from his family.

6:10 Chuck went to school and then to the Queen of Hearts. A waitress there asked him what was the matter—he looked so depressed. He had not noticed his depressed appearance since taking the Thorazine. With the entertainment only topless (because of the new state law banning bottomless shows) the show was not much different, but business was not as good, a waitress told him.

March 9, Friday
Morning.

6:50 I arrived at the apartment. Chuck was awake, dressed, and seated on the sofa. His parents admitted to gaining weight since Christmas. Chuck told them he had lost two pounds.

7:00   In the car Chuck mentioned that this morning he poured hot water into what looked like instant coffee in his cup. The result smelled like bouillon. At first he thought he was hallucinating, but it turned out to be bouillon after all. Chuck told me he dreamed that he became angry at his mother for throwing away his *Playboy* magazines. He went on to say he had slept very well with the Thorazine. This morning when he awakened, his father's face seemed distorted and blackened to him. It took him a while to shake the distortion and to awaken fully.

7:40   We arrived at the Los Angeles International Airport. Chuck dropped off Donna and her baggage and then parked the car. Chuck told me the world seemed "real" to him now. His depth perception seemed better. He wished he could stay in such a condition. We had hot chocolate with Donna and saw her off. Walking back to the car, Chuck heard a voice saying "cream rises to the top."

8:55   After he returned to the apartment, Chuck's speech seemed slurred and he was not alert at times. The Thorazine had not stopped his hallucinations. He felt they might increase before they stopped. His mood seemed elevated slightly, even silly at times. He had selected a book, *Robopaths*, to read.

9:20   As we were eating breakfast, Chuck said something, but his speech was not loud or clear and Jewel misunderstood him. He explained to her why she couldn't hear him well—there are little objects floating in the air, the sounds bounce off them, and the words change. Reasonably enough, she would not accept this explanation of what had happened.

11:40   Mrs. Smith began baking cookies, using the electric mixer and generally making noise. Nevertheless (or *because* she did it), Chuck continued to sleep.

Afternoon.

12:15   Jewel finished the cookies and gave one to me. Chuck was still sleeping. I felt aware of and somewhat angry with her maneuvers, yet I could sympathize with her efforts to "do something for Chuck." I thought that her actions made Chuck rebel and avoid her and try to hurt her in retaliation, but he shared responsibility for his reactions to her. Chuck had become "spongy" inside—eaten away by artificial and indirect solutions to the direct confrontation of an imperfect life situation. It was an easy life that he led. I felt a bit angry at the injustice of it. It probably made his mother angry, also. He was not really expected to be able to work (his mother has stated this explicitly), he had people solicitous of his moods and ideas, he had unlimited free time and lots of unearned money, he had food and shelter, stimulation, love, and various escape routes at hand (books, bars, sleep, medication, television, a large record and tape collection, movies, etc.) should he become bored with his momentary condition.

But he was unhappy, or said he was, and he had convinced himself that it was true. I wanted to believe that he was unhappy because he was unproductive. Such a relationship would fit my own value system that correlates meaningful productivity with life satisfaction, a view rather out-of-fashion but made more reasonable when the definition of productivity is broadened beyond mere economics and business.

12:20   Mrs. Smith said she would fix lunch when Chuck awakened. Then she proceeded to prepare it anyway.

12:35   "I don't know whether to wake him or not. Chuck doesn't like to eat alone. I think I'll wake him up." "Chuck," she said, waking him for lunch. She told him, as one might tell a child, that the food looked delicious.

12:45   As we ate, Jewel spoke proudly of feeding her daughter a big supper the night before despite Donna's protestations that she was trying to lose weight. The pattern was clear. By doing nice things for her children, Mrs. Smith could minimize their self-determination without anyone's awareness or guilt.

12:53   "Come on," Mrs. Smith called me to dessert. I delayed. Chuck had been eating less lately, asking for only one piece of toast in the morning, eating only one sandwich for lunch. He had intentionally lost weight. I predicted that Jewel would pick up on this independent effort of his and would either put him on a diet, as she had in the past, or would fix fattening foods and large helpings in order to encourage him to eat.

1:10   Before leaving for Donna's apartment, Chuck checked on when dinner would be served. As soon as we arrived he lay on the couch. Then he sat, smoked, and drank a beer while listening to Bob Dylan records. He dozed but awakened to flip the record through the first four L.P. sides. By the fifth side, having drunk two cans of beer, he slept through the end of the record and it automatically repeated.

3:40   Chuck lay sprawled on the rug snoring peacefully, one knee up, one arm leaning against the couch like a bird's broken wing.

4:00   The record repeated again.

4:25   Chuck awoke and changed the record.

4:40   Chuck took out the trash and opened a beer. He started to smoke. He knew his parents had planned to eat at 4:30 P.M. He was awake, but he chose not to return.

4:50   The telephone rang. Before answering it Chuck said, "That's my mother." Before she could speak he said, "Hello, Mom. Go ahead. We'll be over in a while." He finished his beer.

5:15   We returned to his parents' apartment and ate supper immediately and quietly.

5:55   Mr. Smith closed the curtains and turned on the television.

7:20   Jewel started to talk just as an interesting television report began. Her husband barked, "Listen!" She shut up.

7:30   His parents considered Chuck to be unable to work or to attend school full time. Mrs. Smith worried that he was ineligible for financial help. When school was out and his G.I. Bill was ended, what would he do? She did not want him to live alone ever again. Mr. Smith believed that if Chuck were "going to do something [suicide]," he would do it whether alone or living with his family. They recalled that whenever Chuck's medication was changed, he slept a lot. His parents did not know what medication he was taking at this time.

7:45   Chuck awoke, checked his watch, and submerged himself again in sleep.

8:20   I made arrangements with the Smiths to call me the next morning as soon as someone was awake. Chuck awoke to say "goodbye." Jewel suggested that he go in to bed.

March 10, Saturday

Morning.

7:40   Chuck telephoned.

7:47   I arrived at the Smiths' apartment. Chuck and Jewel were seated drinking coffee. Jewel noticed that Chuck dropped his cigarette. She commented that he must still be asleep and that she dropped hers, too, sometimes. Jewel asked, "Chuck, what have you got planned?" She inquired whether he wanted to go with her on some errands, but he did not know whether he wanted to or not.

7:55   I asked Chuck how the Thorazine was affecting him. As he started to reply he could not find the right word. Jewel offered, "Relaxed . . . is that the answer you wanted? Relaxed?" He ignored her, stating, "I feel calm." He seemed more alert, with less slurring of speech today. He described a dream from the previous night: Someone was taking pictures with a Polaroid camera. They kept taking photos but not pulling them out of the camera at once. (It seemed to me a good description of our research.) In another dream his brother's wife threw a baby into the water. When it floated down the stream Chuck dived in and rescued it. Someone had told him to dive in so that they could take a photo of him. Jewel described a "distorted, crazy, twisted" dream she had in which Mr. Smith had to drive back East to find work. She was dreading the long drive back East and they were waiting so late to leave. When she awoke, she was glad to be home. In another dream she saw a live grizzly bear inside the gate of a public park. She took a little boy's hand and led him past the bear. The boy was quite happy that she could lead him safely inside.

8:55   Chuck had taken one 100-milligram Thorazine tablet at the hospital on Thursday and two Thorazine tablets Thursday night. He could still feel the effects of the Thorazine more than thirty-six hours later.

9:00   Chuck was lying on the couch, reading. Mr. Smith, seated in the chair, mentioned that Donna was in Spain by then. He and his wife mildly disagreed over what time it was in Spain.

9:05   Mrs. Smith complained that her breakfast looked like the devil. She asked Chuck if he wanted to go on a diet with her and her husband after I left. My earlier prediction about her attempt to exert control over Chuck's weight loss was fulfilled.

9:25   After breakfast, Mr. and Mrs. Smith put back the table and chairs with Jewel directing where each should go.

9:50   Mrs. Smith remarked, "I like being a woman because my husband treats me like a woman." She trusted the *Los Angeles Herald Examiner*. "You can get the truth from the *Examiner*, but the *Times*, they distort everything according to politics."

10:30 Chuck was lying on the couch with Mrs. Smith sitting next to him. She started tickling his foot. He told her to stop but she did not. Finally, he pulled his foot away and halfheartedly kicked at her. At the same time, he jokingly threatened to put ground glass in her hamburger. She laughed but objected, "Chuck, that's too much!"

10:40 Chuck picked up his book. Mrs. Smith began talking, half to herself. She was looking forward to seeing her grandchildren next weekend. She liked living near her children, but she was afraid Donna would move farther away. Such a move would result in inconvenience for the family.

11:05 Mr. Smith had showered and dressed, wearing a bright Hawaiian shirt that caused a bit of stir and several comments. Mr. and Mrs. Smith discussed her grocery list while Chuck continued reading.

11:35 Mrs. Smith told me how good Chuck had looked in the Hawaiian shirt they had bought him. Her focus on Chuck's positive qualities emphasized the past: *he used* to look so good, what he *used to* do that made her proud.

She said she was beginning to feel nervous. She had not felt that way for a long time. Mr. Smith asked if he had anything to do with it. She said she did not think so. Rather, she attributed her nervousness, a kind of tense preoccupation, to having eaten sweets that morning.

Mr. Smith complained about the trash making a mess on the floor as he prepared to take it out. Jewel erupted, "Look at all the times I clean up after you! . . . There, it's all cleaned up. I hope you're satisfied!" Her husband muttered, "Bitch, bitch, bitch," as he walked out with the trash. When he returned, she ordered, "Leave it there; I have to wash it out." "Well, if you'd had a sack in there, you wouldn't need to wash it out." Mrs. Smith shifted ground. "Turn the light on, please." "Why?" " 'Cause I want it on." "Okay." Mr. Smith told her she sure was bossy that morning. She retorted that he started it by being so critical. He argued that he would not be critical if there were not something to criticize. Five minutes later it seemed the fight was over. Then it started up again but was mixed with joking. They stood right up to one another and ended as usual, with a standoff.

11:55 Before leaving for the market, Mr. Smith asked Chuck if he were going, too. "No." "Why?" Chuck replied, "I don't want to go." "Chuck doesn't want to hear our bitching," they laughed. Jewel quipped, "When we get out to the car, he'll hear it." Mr. Smith retorted, "If you see her walking back up here alone, you'll know why." They exited, laughing.

Afternoon.

12:55 Chuck sat smoking, preoccupied. I asked what he had been thinking about. He replied that there were ways in which he felt like a robot—shutting out people and feelings.

1:05 Chuck wrote a note to his parents, "Have gone shopping and to Donna's. Will be back for dinner. Love, Chuck and David."

1:15 At Donna's, Chuck put on a Beatles record, opened a can of beer, and sat at the table, smoking.

1:55 He put on a new tape; the volume was high. Back in his chair at the table, he sat.

2:25 Chuck lay on the couch. I asked him if playing records caused him to recall the days when he worked as a disc jockey. He said "sometimes." Today I was sleepy, having been up until late the night before. Time seemed to pass more quickly as I dozed and dazed through the day. Also, I felt less sensitivity to social cues and pressures, that is, I did not notice or care so much how I acted toward others and how they acted toward me. To doze like this provided defensive padding against "the slings and arrows of outrageous fortune."

4:50 We returned to his parents' apartment. Mrs. Smith was lying on the couch and Mr. Smith was in bed. Chuck wanted dinner. Jewel grinned. "I *said* I bet you'd be starved." She went on trying to make conversation. "You said you might go shopping. What did you buy?" "Nothing."

5:00 Chuck laughed and talked animatedly with his brother Leon on the telephone, being sure to tell him that he was going to college. Chuck also talked with his nephew and niece and seemed to enjoy it. Jewel told Chuck to tell Leon that Donna was in Spain. He did. She hinted, "Don't hang on too long, Chuck."

5:15   Mr. Smith went out for a paper. Chuck was still on the telephone. His eyes looked half-closed, but his speech was clear. He told Leon that the family planned to visit Leon's home next weekend. Mrs. Smith told Chuck to tell Leon that since Charles, Sr., had been working weekends they had not been over to visit. Chuck did not hear or care, so he told Leon that Jewel wanted him to know that "Dad had taken out the garbage or something." He talked to his sister-in-law, too. He told her he had almost killed himself sliding down a snowy mountain last winter, so skiing seemed too hazardous for him. Jewel reminded him to get off the telephone again. He did. Chuck said he planned to pay for the call.

5:20   Jewel pumped Chuck for news from Leon. Chuck responded vaguely and laconically. Then he got up and pulled the table out for dinner.

5:25   Mr. Smith remarked with approval on a newspaper article that mentioned the possibility of bringing back the death penalty and stiff punishments for drug pushers.

5:55   Dinner over, Jewel put the table away. She said, "Chuck, you could've helped me." There was no audible response. Her husband offered, "Honey, you want me to help with that?" Of course, she was finished by then; he knew it, and she knew that he knew it. She berated him, laughing. They read the paper. Jewel read to Chuck a hopeful horoscope about "progress." Her purpose was obvious. He recognized this and made only a minimal, almost sullen response.

6:00   Mrs. Smith began her crossword puzzle. She asked Chuck for a pencil. He was distracted, heard only that she wanted something, and said, "Huh?" She said, "A pencil." He threw one to her, then got up to take his medication.

6:05   Chuck told his parents he was going to Donna's apartment. Jewel told him not to drive if he had a few beers at Donna's. Chuck joked that he would come in at 3:00 A.M. and make a disturbance. This did not set well with his mother. Chuck went to the Queen of Hearts bar. We agreed to meet at Donna's in a few hours. I went to my apartment. I waited at Donna's apartment but soon became worried about Chuck. I drove past his parents' apartment but didn't see his car, so I went to the Queen of Hearts and found him there drinking beer. Perhaps he had drunk seven or eight beers by that time. I stayed for about forty minutes. There were the usual "hello, how are you?" and other short exchanges from the waitresses, aimed at getting Chuck to drink his beer quickly and buy another glass. Chuck had no hallucinations that night. He said that drinking had no effect on his hallucinations. He thought he might come by Donna's apartment that night after leaving the bar. I told him I would leave the door unlocked, and I left.

March 11, Sunday

Morning.

2:15   Chuck arrived at Donna's apartment. He had been dozing at the bar. It had closed at 2:00 A.M. The girls rushed the patrons to hurry their last drinks as closing time approached. Chuck puttered around the kitchen and soon left for his parents' apartment.

6:50   Chuck telephoned. It was pouring rain outside.

7:00   I arrived at his parents' apartment. Mr. Smith had returned from work and was sitting at the table. Chuck was sitting on the couch, drinking coffee. Mrs. Smith was lying in bed. The remains of dinner still sat on the kitchen counter.

7:15   Chuck remained seated on the couch, half dozing. His father emerged from the bathroom and entered the bedroom where Jewel had awakened. He closed the door.

7:20   Chuck slept.

7:50   Jewel got up and brewed coffee. She talked of the one bright spot in her shopping the day before—eggs for 59¢ per dozen. And in great detail she described the gloomier side of her day, feeling sorry for wives with big families and little money. She knew that Chuck had been drinking when he came home early this morning. She wanted to know if he had driven from Donna's apartment.

I silently reflected on Chuck's ability to turn on heartiness and animation with strangers, his brother, fellow patients, and Dr. Harrison, but his drift back into the comfortable, habitual, depressive defense at home.

8:10 Mrs. Smith thought that living at home might not be good for Chuck. But she thought board-and-care facilities were bad for him. She seemed to think that he was doing well when he first came home, but once he started drinking "he becomes another person altogether." Jewel wondered, "What are we going to do?" I told her the social worker was thinking about inviting Chuck back to the hospital if the changed medication did not work out. The conversation was carried on very softly beside Chuck's sleeping form. His toes were jerking spasmodically.

8:15 Mrs. Smith arose and went to the kitchen. Chuck got up. His mother called out, "Good morning." "Good morning."

8:20 Jewel sat in her chair, smoking. "What do you two want for breakfast?" Then, "This house smelled strong when you came home. It woke me up. I had to get up and open a window." She went on, "Oh, Chuck! That's so dangerous! You should have stayed over at Donna's and made yourself a pallet." She changed the subject, or did she? She talked about liking their previous apartment's ventilation. But the manager there was a drunk, the man upstairs was a drunk, and the people across the way were drunks who fought.

8:35 Jewel laughed as she criticized her husband for blowing wax over the table last night when he blew out the dinner candles. She exclaimed, "He's something else!" But despite the laughter, the constant complaints and criticisms remained acrid and pervasive.

8:55 Chuck cleared off the breakfast table. Jewel asked him to close the door to the bedroom so that his father could continue to sleep undisturbed. She rambled on about their trips to Las Vegas and Europe. As usual, the delightful, happy experiences were overshadowed by disappointments— pictures that failed to turn out, rain, closed museums. "We were crushed. It just made you sick." On and on. . . .

9:05 Jewel hoped Donna would not lose the camera she had borrowed from a co-worker for her trip. Chuck said, "Bill sure is a nice guy." Mrs. Smith noted that Bill needed other people to like him but that he was often rejected by other people. "Some people won't talk to ordinary people because of snobbery." Chuck agreed, "They have something wrong with them." I noted that the focus of attention had shifted from a "nice guy" to "defective people" who have "something wrong with them." Chuck began again, "Perkins is a nice guy." Jewel axed this seedling, too. "He doesn't have any children and tries to make up for it by being a clown for the children at parties." She continued, "The chairman of the board (at the taxi company) is a person I thoroughly dislike! I can't stand that man!"

9:15   Chuck was lying on the couch. Mrs. Smith was seated in the chair with her head in her hands, the picture of depression. Then her hands covered her face, her head still bowed. Chuck watched her silently. Finally, she shook herself into action. "Well, I've got to get this kitchen straightened up." She moved to the kitchen. Chuck was lying wriggling his toes.

9:40   Jewel opened the door "because the room is stuffy and smoke filled." Chuck said he could not wait until summer so that he could go swimming in the pool downstairs. He mentioned that Leon believed himself and Chuck to be dumbbells compared to Donna, who had already traveled a lot at her young age. Mrs. Smith responded that Leon and Chuck were not dumbbells, but that Donna was more aggressive. She considered that for Leon "the sky's the limit" occupationally. She could not understand why he continued to resist the promotions his department offered him. He said he did not want the added responsibility, even though there was a salary increase involved.

Chuck mused, "Sometimes I think it's a miracle that people live as long as they do with disease, car wrecks, and things like that." Jewel responded, "There's no use thinking about it. . . . " Chuck faced her. "It's okay to think about it if you don't dwell on it. . . . Every time I get on the freeway I get a twinge of fear." "We all do; that's normal. . . . We can always get another car but we can't get another Chuck." Chuck looked serious. "Oh, you don't need a Chuck anyway." She lectured him on drinking and driving. He poured himself a glass of Kool-Aid.

10:35   "There's one pleasant thing about the rain," Mrs. Smith offered. "I haven't heard the ambulance flying by every minute." Her voice, though lively, carried tones of weariness and resignation. Chuck spoke of the rain resulting in a construction delay at the research labs at the hospital. His mother acknowledged that "the holes will fill up and they'll have to pump them out."

10:40 Occasionally Chuck read a passage or shared an idea from an article with his mother. She seemed to understand; she asked sensible questions. Chuck finished his article. He told Jewel that his Thorazine was to be taken only when he could not sleep. The doctor had told him he could take up to two at night. Mrs. Smith told him he did not get enough exercise and he slept a lot during the daytime, so it was no wonder that he could not sleep at night. He reminded her that sometimes he did not sleep at all during the day.

11:00 Jewel asked Chuck to get her a newspaper because the rain had stopped for the moment. "I don't want to, but I will." He reached for his shoes and socks, put them on, and left.

11:05 Chuck returned with the paper. "Thank you." "You're welcome." The polite amenities were not forgotten in this family.

Mrs. Smith was smoking quite a bit more at this time than a couple of weeks ago. Suddenly Chuck remarked, "One of the guys up at the hospital was doing well, got out, got an apartment, got married, and then a couple of days later he cut his wrists." Jewel exclaimed, "Oh Chuck!" He reassured her, "They got him in time though."

11:30 Mrs. Smith started up another conversation with her dozing son. The newspaper contained an ad for volunteers. Jewel suggested that she and Chuck go down once per week to help in a residential-care facility for the mentally disturbed. Chuck seemed to be interested. They talked of what they could do. Chuck dryly commented, "That might be fun! The blind leading the blind." He quoted Dr. Murray Banks, who said that people become depressed when they lose interest in life. "There's a lot of truth in that." They seemed doubtful about what to offer the mentally disturbed residents. I suggested that listening was important, and anyone could do that. They considered the empathy and understanding Chuck would have with these people. But Mrs. Smith warned him not to get attached to the people there, like they did at the nursing home she used to manage. "When someone is sensitive enough it's easy to drive them crazy," said Chuck, "All you have to do is find a weak spot and pick at it and pretty soon they'll crack."

Afternoon.

12:45 Charles, Sr., got up. Jewel hugged him and offered him coffee. From the couch, Chuck mentioned that whenever a truck passed or any other vibration caused the apartment to rattle, he feared another earthquake was starting.

12:55 "Your hair sure looks pretty, Mama," Chuck praised her and Jewel responded, "Thanks, Chuck. I didn't even brush it today." "It just shines!"

I felt that the Smith family had pretty much accustomed themselves to my sitting in the same chair writing or reading nearly all the time. Because I wrote letters, corrected manuscripts, and took notes throughout the day, and because I often delayed a minute or more before recording what had transpired, the Smith family had no sense of when I was writing about them and when I was not.

1:50 Mrs. Smith sighed, "Well, well, well." Mr. Smith looked up. "That's a deep subject." Jewel beat him to the punch, " . . . for such a shallow mind?" "You said that; I didn't." They laughed. Chuck told a joke about a man reading in the bottom of a swimming pool. He was studying "in depth." There was more laughter. His father appreciated the joke, "That was a good one, Chuck." Soon Chuck appeared to be asleep on the couch, but his responses to noises and questions demonstrated that he was awake.

2:00 Chuck remarked on the beautiful sky today. Rich blue was showing between white, shining clouds.

2:15 He got up, turned on the radio very low, sat, and smoked. Charles, Sr., emerged. "Gee, I couldn't hear that radio before I went into the bathroom." He laughed that washing his ears again must have helped his hearing.

2:40 Jewel cajoled her spouse into dressing up to visit a family friend. They changed clothes and left.

3:05 Chuck put down his book and went to sleep on the couch. The facade of reading was no longer necessary.

5:55 After dinner, Mr. Smith caught Jewel in a couple of her attempts to manipulate him. For example, he asked straight-faced, "Honey, are you trying to get me to say you've still got a good figure?" Charles, Sr., kept the conversation light with his dry humor and puns. He continued hurling compliments at Mrs. Smith, but the tone was so dry that it was obvious they were insincere. If she reacted to the tone, he asked her what he had *said* to upset her. Thus, when it was convenient for him, he emphasized the words instead of the tone. Then he played humble, with hurt innocence, again drily. Sometimes the hostility surfaced through the humor and both arched their backs verbally, snapping an exchange or two, but Mr. Smith slid into humor immediately and the anger evaporated or slipped underneath again.

6:05   Chuck was seated on the couch, with his chin resting on clasped hands, rocking slightly; his coffee was nearby. Mr. Smith sat in a chair reading the newspaper. Mrs. Smith, having finished in the kitchen, lit a cigarette.

8:25   Chuck was lying on the pallet in the bedroom, awake, listening to Donovan tapes. On the dresser were his four bottles of medications: Artane, 2 mg., 1 tablet 2 times daily; Elavil, 25 mg., 1 tablet in the A.M. and, if needed, 1 tablet in the P.M.; Stelazine, 10 mg., 1 tablet 3 times daily; and Thorazine, 100 mg., 1 tablet at noon for hyperactivity and 1 or 2 tablets at bedtime for insomnia as needed.

8:40   Jewel brought in ice cream and cookies topped with fruit cocktail.

8:45   Chuck took the dishes to rinse in the kitchen. Then he lay back on the pallet, smoking.

9:45   Chuck got up to take his medicine. He lay back down and smoked a cigarette. He noticed that I had written over 100 pages of notes already. He asked if all of the journal would be published. I guessed that only excerpts and a summary were ever likely to be in print. Soon Chuck was asleep.

March 12, Monday

Morning.

6:50   Chuck was still asleep, though his parents were up. Jewel thought she had Chuck's mood change figured out. The previous day was comparatively good, except for his sleeping, because Chuck did not drink. Alcohol is a depressant, so she felt that when Chuck drank he became depressed. As simple as that.

7:40 Chuck moved from bedroom to coffee to couch.

7:45 Jewel hoped that no one in her family ever got cancer like the friend they had visited yesterday. She added that she would be glad when the weather warmed up so she could air out the house. It all smelled bad—smoke, food odors, her hair. (Illness, death, and bad smells—good morning!)

8:02 "Even with the light on in here, this is such a dismal kitchen," Jewel said to no one in particular.

8:10 Jewel again tried to find out the duration of the break between semesters and whether Chuck planned to go to school during the summer. Her son gave short, uninformative, noncommittal, disinterested replies.

8:15 Chuck was lying awake on the couch. Mrs. Smith threw a towel at him. "You missed," he said, throwing it back at her. He missed, too.

8:25 We ate breakfast. Again, Chuck delayed coming to the table. Jewel asked if he wanted to help her on a crafts project. He told her he planned to work on his paper that day at Donna's apartment. She said that his studies came first, so they would work on the chair another time. She extolled the virtues of Donna's apartment for studying. (She had told me while Chuck was asleep that she wanted us out of the Smiths' apartment so she could clean.)

8:55 Jewel said that her husband was brought up to expect three hot meals per day. "I put a stop to that right quick. At least he's understanding." While she talked, Chuck got up and left the room.

9:00 Jewel and I discussed her smoking. X-rays showed she had only a few nicotine stains in her lungs. "You see, my lungs are strong and fight it." There was a general admiration in this family for properly directed strength and aggressiveness. Weakness was seen as a symptom of mental and physical dysfunction.

9:05 Chuck emerged from the bedroom, dressed. Mrs. Smith sat with her forehead in her hand. "What's the matter, Mama?" "Oh, I'm just relaxing a bit. Nothing wrong," she responded wearily. She straightened up in the chair and hummed a soft tune but continued to appear lost in her thoughts. Here sat the living model for someone's concealed, denied depression.

9:10 Chuck seemed in no hurry to leave for Donna's place. Probably the delay was because he sensed his mother's eagerness for us to go. Jewel complained that she was "taking a cold."

9:12 Chuck asked, "What time do the banks open, 9 A.M. or 10 A.M.?" Mrs. Smith thought it was 9 A.M. She wondered why he asked. Chuck had two checks he wanted to put in a savings account. "Good idea."

9:13 Chuck lay back on the couch. Mrs. Smith sat with her head propped on her hand and stared at the floor, stalemated by her son's immobility.

9:15 We left for the bank.

Afternoon.

12:30 Chuck discovered he needed some typing paper, so we went to the drugstore. Chuck noticed some Viewmaster slide sets entitled "Hearst Castle" and "Exploring the Universe." He impulsively bought them as well as the paper he had originally intended to buy. He complained that Elavil was altering his perception of reality, making him see objects as more distant than they were.

12:45 We returned to the Smiths' apartment. Chuck sat and looked at the slides. Jewel read the paper, waiting her turn. She impatiently told Chuck to hurry up. Then she sat placidly, turned away, and read.

1:00 Chuck turned the viewer over to her, saying, "David is next." He got up to make coffee. As she peered through the viewer, Mrs. Smith reminisced about the trip she and her husband had made to the Hearst Castle.

1:45 Jewel took her medication fifteen minutes early so she would not forget.

1:50 Chuck set an old desk-model Smith-Corona typewriter on the desk in the living room and began to type his paper.

1:55 The typewriter keys were sticking, so he decided to write out the paper in longhand. His writing was neat and legible. He playfully ran his finger up Jewel's backbone as he passed her in the kitchen. Then they threw a wadded-up cigarette package back and forth at each other. "You're as mean as your Daddy!" she smiled. Chuck's spirits seemed high.

2:40 Jewel sighed, "Wow, I'm tired again. I just wouldn't be able to hold a regular job and I know it." It had become hot and stuffy in the room. I opened the door a crack.

2:45 Jewel offered Chuck a taste of the cabbage heart she was eating. He accepted but said he couldn't taste anything. She chided him; his taste buds must be dead. She did not accept his evaluation of the taste as valid *for him*.

3:15 Jewel asked Chuck if he planned to shower that night. He said he did and asked why. She replied that she planned to take one that night also.

3:17 Chuck returned to writing. Jewel sat pensively in the rocking chair, smoking. Her pile of crochet yarn lay untouched on her lap for fifteen minutes.

4:15 Mr. Smith went into the kitchen for nuts. Jewel ran him out of there, but not until he had snatched some. He headed for the couch and the paper. Jewel sang, "Make the World Go Away." Chuck asked, "Why? To get it off of your shoulders?" The parents joined in playful fighting while Jewel set the table.

4:50 Chuck decided to go to Donna's apartment. Jewel told him that dessert—jello and ice cream—would be served about 8:30 P.M. Of course, we knew she could serve it anytime; we knew also that she wanted us back by then.

4:55 Chuck stopped at the liquor store for a six-pack of beer. He asked the store salesman, "Think it'll rain tonight?" "No, we close at 10 P.M. on Saturday and Sunday," was the strange reply. (Chuck called this kind of response "robotic"; the clerk was "programmed" to emit closing hours so he had not listened to the question.)

5:50 At Donna's, Chuck got up for another beer and returned to the floor to listen to a Simon and Garfunkel tape. He asked what I would like to hear. I sidestepped the decision, commenting that sidestepping would be necessary for a while longer. Chuck decided, "We'll put on a little acid rock now." I had mentioned several weeks ago that I didn't like acid rock, but said "okay." The music began. It was classical. Chuck smiled.

7:20 Chuck sat and listened, half dozing in the darkened room except when he got up a few times to go to the bathroom.

7:24 Chuck informed me that, "A voice just called me a 'capitalist pig.' "
7:26 Chuck lay asleep. The music stopped. He awoke and played a cassette containing electronic music of the Moog synthesizer. (At the hospital, a nurse who had worked with Chuck had heard it played on his tape recorder, noting in his record that the music was depressing. It certainly was not. It was strange but lively and happy.)
8:00 Chuck called my attention to the "canned" applause at the end of the Moog performance. How appropriate—artificial applause for artificial music! He had another beer.
9:35 Chuck telephoned his parents to tell them he would be home early. Then he walked straight to the couch, lay down, and went to sleep.
9:40 The music ended. He got up and turned on the radio. He went back to sleep on the couch. The room was chilly.
10:00 I slipped away to pick up mail. Chuck did not know that I had been gone when I told him the next day.
10:40 He was asleep as before when I returned.
10:55 I turned on the heater and covered Chuck with two blankets. That night I felt fear for my safety while sleeping with Chuck in the same apartment. So I closed Donna's bedroom door (it had noisily jangling bells on it) and went to bed. After a short while, I fell asleep. On reflection, I was not sure what prompted the fear. Perhaps it was merely the product of my imagination, but I felt a strain in my relationship with Chuck and a genuine concern that he would not hesitate to harm me that night. But nothing unusual transpired.

March 13, Tuesday

Morning.

4:35 Chuck awoke and went to the bathroom. Then he turned on the kitchen light, drank some Dr. Pepper, and smoked a cigarette. He tried to go back to sleep but could not.
5:00 Chuck turned the kitchen light on again, prepared a pot of coffee, and sat at the table in the dawning light. He sipped coffee and smoked.

5:15   Bob Dylan sang/spoke his piercing commentaries from the phonograph.

5:45   Chuck played the other side of the record, folded the blankets, put them away, washed out his cup, lit a cigarette, and lay dozing in front of the speakers.

7:00   The cuckoo clock sounded. "Right on time, bird," Chuck snapped.

7:05   Chuck played a tape by Melanie, "The Id Goes Marching On." He considered it his song. "Too much!" he commented. His mood seemed fairly bright this morning.

7:20   He rocked back and forth to another song by Melanie, whistling. This lengthy playing of music by Chuck seemed to be an effort to make time pass. By playing music, Chuck could escape from his mother and fill time until his class, until his glasses were ready, until the check arrived, until the alcohol took effect, until he died. He had managed to implant extra meaning into music by memorizing lyrics and by building sensuous associations to the melody through watching the women perform at the nude bar.

Afternoon.

12:55   We returned to the apartment after shopping. Chuck promptly began playing his new phonograph records.

2:05   Chuck slept. His mother predicted that he would sleep until 4:30 or 5:00 P.M.

4:05   Chuck's father returned from work. In a short while, he emerged from the bedroom in casual clothes. He sat on the couch reading the newspaper. Mrs. Smith told me that her husband didn't want Chuck to have a car. If Chuck hurt someone after drinking "that would be the end of him." She worried that he would be unable to get a job with his history of mental illness. She was afraid to think of what might happen to Chuck if anything should happen to his parents. "I just don't know what he's going to do."

4:16   A telephone call for Chuck ended his nap.

4:50   We ate dinner while watching news on television. Chuck appeared disinterested in the special news item concerning nude bars. His mother complained of the minimal amounts of meat and vegetables in her frozen meat pie.

That evening Chuck and I attended a group at the V.A.,

accompanied his friend on a visit to a woman's apartment, and drank at McGinty's Pub on Wilshire Boulevard well into the night.

March 14, Wednesday
Morning.

7:35 Mr. and Mrs. Smith planned to travel around the U.S. in a camper when they retired. Jewel advised, "So, Son, you'll have to straighten yourself up or plan to go with us. We don't want you dangling in midair. . . . But by then, maybe they'll come up with something to help people in your condition."

8:00 Chuck got up to take his medicine. He swung his arms for exercise and poured another cup of coffee.

8:30 Chuck informed us that sometimes he was not paying attention to the conversation because he was running music through his mind. After three years as a disc jockey with earphones on he had heard a lot of music. Jewel noted that earphones, jet noises, and other loud sounds can ruin one's hearing. She praised her own "superhearing."

8:35 Jewel sat for a moment, resting. "This is not getting my house cleaned." She popped up and went into the kitchen. From there she told Chuck she didn't appreciate his calling her a "devil" this morning. She laughed and asked what I thought of that. I said it depended on how he said it. "David just won't commit himself. . . . He just won't become involved," she smiled knowingly. Chuck interjected, "A lot of people are feeling better now, now that the war is over and the prisoners are coming home." Was he speaking of Viet Nam?

8:45 While washing dishes, Jewel mentioned bringing dolls to her granddaughter from the places they visited on their trips. Chuck suggested that "out of one's *senses*" was a more apt descriptive phrase than "out of one's *mind*," because when a person was disturbed he was very much into his mind but withdrawn from sensory input. He wrote this idea in his small notebook to be used later in the book he works on sporadically. It started out to be a quickly jotted note, but ideas kept coming so he continued writing for some twenty minutes.

9:15 Chuck showed his notes to me. Jewel asked to see them. We discussed with satisfaction his expression of his feelings in writing. He wrote that trying to hold on to good feelings was a poor substitute for feeling deeply and letting feelings flow. He also wrote that play was good in itself (a carryover from his social worker's counsel the previous night).

Chuck's notes entitled "Pardon My Psychosis" ended with "God Bless You." Jewel emphasized how lucky Chuck was to come home to a family's love. I stressed that Chuck's security was in himself and not in his family or in the hospital. Mrs. Smith noted that if she or her husband's "mind breaks" they would not have the resources that Chuck has as a veteran. I praised Chuck for recognizing the usefulness of expressing his insights to others. I urged him to have many small goals in addition to his big one of publishing a great book some day.

Jewel maintained her cautious, not-daringly-hopeful stance; she exuded a little girl's wishfulness that life would go well. But the tremulous hope came with a hard expectation that life might not go well.

10:20 Chuck rocked back and forth on the couch. The living room was overcast with cigarette clouds.

10:40 Mrs. Smith, dressed neatly and with fresh makeup, stood in front of Chuck, ready for shopping. When Chuck got up to go, she puttered around forcing him to wait.

10:45 At the market, Chuck waited in the car listening to the radio while Jewel shopped.

11:00 On the way to the lumber yard, Jewel criticized modern singers. She hated Bob Dylan. Chuck said he liked some and he did not like some. As we waited again in the car, I remarked favorably on his ability to be precise in his speech, resisting absolutism. I noted aloud how such extreme thinking can precede suicide. He agreed.

11:35 Jewel began work on her latest craft project. Chuck rose immediately and made Kool-Aid. Chuck noted, "They didn't have grape or cherry Kool-Aid." Jewel responded, "They're getting pretty slack about that Kool-Aid." "Or else grape and cherry are their most popular flavors," Chuck offered an alternative possibility.

12:00 Mrs. Smith worked on her project. "Aren't you going to study today, Chuck?" "After a while." She made several mistakes while doing her domestic chores. "I don't know what I'm thinking about today." "What's on your mind?" Chuck wondered. "I don't know, Chuck."

Afternoon.

12:15 Jewel threw down the screwdriver. "What's the matter?" "Nothing's going right!" She looked despondent.

12:30 Jewel sat smoking in a chair while Chuck listened to a Bob Dylan tape in the bedroom. He reminded his mother to take her medication. She thanked him.

1:00 Jewel spoke as if Chuck were sitting up awake although he appeared to be sleeping. "You know, these pickles are good." After a pause, Chuck responded clearly.

1:05 Mrs. Smith sat working on a crossword puzzle.

1:10 She suggested, "Why don't you two go into the bedroom. The manager will drop in soon, and it'll be yak, yak, yak." There was a pause and no movement. "You'll rest better." Still Chuck did not move. I looked his way, hesitating to make any move until he did.

1:15 He took out the trash. "You want to shut the door, Chuck? The wind comes up this time of the afternoon." On his return he went into the bedroom. A few minutes later she called out her thanks for his taking out the trash.

3:15 Jewel had invited Leon's family for dinner. They were on their way. She hoped Leon had not been drinking. He had wanted to bring beer for supper, but she had talked him into bringing only one can for himself.

3:35 The Smith family together, we ate a snack and then dinner amid much talk. Embracing and verbal expressions of love were accepted and expected. On this occasion, Chuck was the quietest member of the family. Jewel kept telling Leon that his voice was too loud and that he should be more quiet. Leon's two older children played with toys that were kept at the Smith apartment. The baby was held and fed. Jewel exclaimed over the beauty of the two youngest children. Everyone seemed surprised that the eldest child was at the top of her class. Perhaps she was being selected as a second-generation focus for family difficulties, as Chuck had been in his generation. Chuck was the "accepted" sick member of the family, a role both he and his family expected him to play.

Leon shared his parents' concern with money. For example, he told us several times that the barbecued meat he had bought for the meal cost $5.30. His self-praise was subtler than Jewel's. It resulted in a one-up exchange with his mother about the places they had seen in their travels.

Leon freely talked in general terms of the arguments he had with his wife. He hinted that his marriage (like others in our time and society) was shaky, that he and his wife were held together strongly by their children. Leon reported that his wife considered him an alcoholic, but he disagreed because he could go for two to three days without alcohol and no withdrawal symptoms appeared. He admitted his addiction to cigarettes, however. Leon was a dynamic, pressured person who needed approval. He described himself as a worrier. Jewel consistently tried to control and maneuver him. He skillfully found some sort of compromise that permitted him autonomy without antagonizing his mother. He highly praised the Smith family and the security he had felt as a child. This account seemed somewhat incongruent with Chuck's stories of his parents' alcoholism and other family troubles during his childhood.

The Smith grandparents, Jewel and Charles, Sr., showed the doting patience, the joyful affection for their grandchildren that one sees anywhere. Jewel appeared to worry excessively about her grandchildren and was sometimes sharp with them. She would speak warmly and lovingly one moment, then unexpectedly she would call out sharply to a child who was misbehaving or near potential danger. The contrast in vocal tone was startling to me and must have been even more so to the children. Was this a source of Chuck's voices?

On the whole, however, the family showed a warm closeness that offered genuine security and tolerance for the mild idiosyncracies of its members.

5:50 After Leon's family left, the Smiths talked about his loud voice. Jewel said he had always been that way.

6:05 Prepared to leave, Chuck was sidetracked by an antenna problem with the television set. Mr. and Mrs. Smith spatted over her effort to fix the picture by means forbidden in the instructions. "Do it yourself!" she snapped. But control was not relinquished so easily. She returned to the set and finally adjusted it so that the picture was fairly clear.

March 15, Thursday

Morning.

8:05 While Chuck continued to sleep, his mother vented some feelings about his lying around. "We can't build our lives around Chuck!" She said her husband thought Chuck was "lazy," that he would be "like he is" until he got up "off his butt." They did not plan to move to accommodate Chuck. They could afford to move, she made it clear, but would not. She was embarrassed by the impression Chuck made as he lay on the couch with the curtains open. Anyone who walked by could see him. From now on if he wanted to sleep, she had decided, it would be in the bedroom. I told her to talk directly with Chuck about these matters. She planned to wait about a week after our research was over to see how Chuck got along before checking into the volunteer work they had discussed earlier.

8:15 Jewel awakened her son. "Chuck, breakfast is going to be ready in a minute and I don't want you to eat old, cold bacon." As Chuck got up, Jewel continued to prepare breakfast. She hummed, feeling somewhat better after expressing some of her angry thoughts.

8:40 Jewel asked Chuck if he would help shampoo Donna's carpet. He replied in a soft voice that he would. Later she asked again. "I said I would." She laughed saying she only wanted reassurance. Then she made the point that Chuck was the tallest and biggest of her children.

9:05 Chuck still sat on the couch, engrossed in his thoughts. He was mildly indignant at the amount of time it was taking to have his glasses made. "It's ridiculous!" he murmured.

9:15 Chuck lay on the couch. Jewel said nothing to him about his being there in view of passersby, despite her complaints to me.

9:37 Chuck went out for the mail. "As big and heavy as he is you still can't hear him going down the stairs." She was convinced that other people had no excuse for making so much noise.

9:52   Jewel maneuvered Chuck into getting ready to leave for Donna's, but when he was finally up and moving, she decided she had to have something to eat.

9:55   Chuck stood in the bedroom, looking at himself in the mirror. Mrs. Smith sat in her chair and ate cereal. Chuck wandered back into the living room. He sat in a dinette chair. "Everyone's going somewhere but me." Jewel pointed out that while Chuck was in school, he could not go anywhere. She said that Leon felt the same way, but when his children "are grown and independent, he and his wife can take off."

10:05   At Donna's apartment Jewel took over, as expected. She directed and fussed until our results suited her discriminating eye. Chuck did the vacuuming and shampooing. I changed the linen with Jewel's "help." She put away the laundry. Chuck flared up at her once for her controlling behavior.

10:55   As we drove back, Jewel tried to get Chuck to pull into a particular driveway, to turn around, and then to wait for a car to pull out so he could park in that vacated space. He didn't follow her advice, however, and told her not to worry about such things.

11:00   Jewel sat on the sofa and stared at the ceiling for a moment. Then she went into the kitchen to begin warming lunch. Chuck emerged from the bedroom to take a Thorazine tablet. Jewel probed, "What's the matter, Chuck?" "I'm all tied up in knots."

      Later, Jewel told me that she had felt tied up in knots on the previous day and her husband had felt that way, too. She said that they knew what to do about tension to get their minds off it, but Chuck worried. She expressed her fears that this sort of nervousness had preceded Chuck's last hospitalization. Nothing that happened or was said or done precipitated that return to the hospital either, she believed. This time, however, she was somewhat relieved to know that Chuck could recognize a relapse when it was approaching.

11:20   As we ate lunch, Chuck complained of nervousness and a burning sensation in his stomach.

11:35   The Thorazine began to take effect. Chuck was calming down, and his stomach felt better. "It's getting to the point where almost everything you do is wrong these days." He explained that, for example, certain foods are not good for you.

11:40   From the couch, Chuck chatted with Jewel. She spoke of the plans for the three of them to go on various trips. She planned to go to the snow and "beat the pants off" Chuck in a snowball fight. Chuck called her a tomboy. He told her he still loved her ... she smiled ... "a little bit." She laughed, "You take all the joy out of life!" They reminisced about his childhood years. "That seemed like a thousand years ago." She sat in her chair and finished a cigarette.

      Chuck mentioned that Leon called him Rasputin because of his hair and beard. Rasputin was assassinated; maybe he, too, would be assassinated. Jewel laughed uncomfortably, "Oh, Chuck!" She wanted him to stop that sort of talk.

11:50   The conversation turned to hippies. Chuck remarked, "All you have to do is find something new, and pretty soon it'll be contaminated by people." Mrs. Smith agreed, "It becomes dirt." A moment later she inquired, "Will you see the doctor today, Chuck?" "Mmm hmm, I'm going to tell him I'm getting nervous again." She thought that was a good idea and told him she, too, had felt that way yesterday.

11:53   Jewel took her medicine.

Afternoon.

 2:35   At the V.A. hospital Chuck met with Dr. Raphael, his psychiatrist. Chuck told him that everything was beautiful one moment and then everything became dark, like heaven and hell. The doctor wanted to know if this happened often. Chuck said it happened many times a day. The doctor gave unclear instructions (which Chuck could not repeat later) on the basis of misinformation from Chuck about the kinds of medication he had been taking (actually, he had not been taking them).

      Chuck's hallucinations were unusual in that they were visual and under some imaginative control, but he used the term "hallucination" as if both he and the doctor knew precisely what he was talking about.

 3:30   Chuck was comparatively quiet during Dr. Harrison's group-therapy session. As usual, he accompanied her to her car.

5:00 On his former ward, the social worker quizzed Chuck and decided to invite him back to the hospital. If he became upset over the weekend, he could come and sleep on the ward. She arranged to call him as soon as there was an empty bed for him. She asked how Chuck's parents would accept his coming back into the hospital. Chuck said his parents would be a little depressed, but if he had to come. . . .

Chuck described an illusion from the previous night in which he saw his professor as a playing card, appropriately tall and wide but with no depth. He rocked back and forth. Perhaps he was trying to assure his safe retreat to the haven of his ward. His money was running out. He was tired of being home.

At this point, I believed I sensed some of the possible causes of his sudden perceptual changes: his voices and his visual hallucinations. The shift from light to dark seemed to parallel Jewel's speech patterns: positive topics followed by negative, gloomy ones. The critical voices and the controlling voices carried the same tone as is commonly encountered in the Smith household. The visual illusions and hallucinations probably resulted from some combination of a readily excitable imagination and the psychochemical drugs (including alcohol) that Chuck was taking.

While we walked to the car, Chuck remarked how passive and nondirective I was. I told him that he had enough controllers and manipulators in his world, that he did not need another one. He said that he realized his mother was very controlling and dominating.

7:35 At the community college, Chuck recalled that the last time he withdrew from school was just before he attempted suicide. He took care of the business of withdrawing. He chatted easily with the clerk while doing so. On the form, he checked as reasons for withdrawing: "Course content not what I expected" and "Personal problems." He felt it was a relief to drop the classes, a weight eased off his mind.

8:10 As we crossed the busy street in front of the college, several students were picking up typed pages that appeared to have blown out of their car window. My impulse was to help them as the traffic waited. But Chuck merely called a greeting and passed on.

8:30 Although I had planned to spend the night at my apartment, Chuck seemed to want me to stay at his place that night. He asked if I still planned to go home. I told him I would go home, break my date, and return to the bar at 11 P.M. He was to wait there for me.

10:50 Chuck was nowhere to be found, though his car was parked outside the Queen of Hearts. I worried about having left him alone even for a short time that night. Eventually, I found Chuck asleep in the back seat of his car. I awakened him and followed him home.

11:00 We arrived at the Smiths' apartment. Chuck's parents greeted him in a friendly, sleepy manner.

11:05 Chuck made a cheese sandwich. He helped me prepare a sleeping area, took his medicine, and went to bed.

March 16, Friday

Morning.

7:45 Jewel wondered why I had returned with Chuck the night before. I evaded her questions, telling her Chuck would fill her in on his activities. She argued that one couldn't tell a mother not to worry (I hadn't); it's foolishness. "I try to make life as easy for him as I possibly can," she lamented.

7:55 Jewel made her bed and straightened up the bedroom. Chuck remained asleep. He dreamed he was a four-star general. Perhaps the stars symbolized his previous four hospital admissions.

8:05 Jewel said to herself, "Well, I got that done. Thank goodness." She had trouble holding her match still, "Can't even light a cigarette this morning."

8:10 Jewel proudly showed me the shelves she had completed. She gleefully added a vignette from last night in which her husband had thought it would take her all night to clean up the mess she had made while potting some plants. She had done it quickly and had proved him wrong.

8:11 Chuck awoke and came in for coffee. "Did the doctor take you off that medicine?" He told her they would try spansules. "You know what? You're going to have to take out the trash today or we're going to have to move."

8:20 "I'm late. You're slipping. You didn't remind me to take my medicine today, Chuck . . . You don't know how lucky you are. You don't have to pay for your medicine." Then Jewel criticized herself for breaking the eggs as she turned them over in the frying pan.

8:30 After breakfast, Chuck started to get the trash together. Jewel jumped up to supervise and help him. He told her *he* was doing it. She realized her attempted control. "Here you're a grown man and Mama still treats you like a little boy." She promised that someday she would get over treating him that way. "Won't you be glad when I do?" "It doesn't matter."

9:00 Chuck's spirits seemed pretty high as he sat talking about the rescues he had made as a lifeguard. Jewel praised his strength in the past.

9:10 Jewel glanced up. "Oh, Chuck's asleep." "No, I'm not."

9:48 Within minutes of Jewel's departure, Chuck got up and poured a glass of Kool-Aid. Often his reading seemed to be a "front" to keep his mother believing that he was occupied. This hypothesis was supported by the ease with which he put his book down and slipped into sleep or other pastimes when she left. Similarly, school provided an acceptable answer to those who asked what he was doing with himself. He could say vaguely, with some pride, that he was going to college. When pinned down, however, he would honestly admit that each class took only a couple of hours of preparation each week and one evening each of class time.

10:05 Chuck showed me a black and white card that, when spun on a phonograph turntable, gradually took on colors. He was fascinated by illusions. Then he put on a Bob Dylan record and sat in the bedroom, smoking and listening. Unexpectedly, he appeared with a camera and took a photograph of me.

10:15 Jewel returned, exhilarated from being out on such a fine day. Chuck caught himself rocking back and forth and stopped.

10:27 Chuck rose to answer the telephone. In some respects, his life was geared to his reacting to the moment. He lived to respond. On the telephone his social worker advised him that a bed had been arranged for him at the hospital. He hummed happily. After hanging up, he showed me two holes he had burned in his shirt. "I must be nuts for smoking."

10:32 Chuck started to pack a grocery bag. He still had not said anything to his mother about returning to the hospital. Thoughtfully, he selected the books he was going to take.

10:37 "I'm sure I'm going to forget something." He hummed, moving purposefully and lightly about the room as he gathered and straightened out his belongings. He was obviously pleased to be going back to the hospital.

10:45 Chuck started to walk out with his bag and clothes. He mentioned casually that he was going back to the hospital. Jewel expressed her concern and love. She recalled that her rug-cleaning machine was in Chuck's car trunk. Would he take it out before leaving?

11:25 On his former ward, Chuck was greeted by the staff.

11:30 As Chuck put fresh linen on his bed another patient came in and greeted him.

11:38 The social worker at admissions had Chuck wait five minutes, then referred him to a second social worker. There seemed to be some question as to whether Chuck was still on outpatient status.

11:50 He waited in the admissions waiting room and smoked. "They're probably drawing straws to see where I'm going to go."

12:00 The first social worker told him to go back to his ward, that he did not need to go through this procedure after all. Chuck joked that this hospital is the best hotel in town.

Afternoon.

12:25 Having returned from lunch, Chuck sat and talked with his ward social worker. "Perhaps we can go sit outside the doctor's office and look pitiful." She spoke of the problem of getting Chuck officially admitted to her ward. She noted they had to be careful of the image that Chuck was to present. If Chuck appeared too sick, then he would go to a locked ward; if he were only slightly ill, then he would return to his desired ward; if he were not sick at all, then no readmission.

1:30 Chuck had been waiting for half an hour to be examined by

Dr. Raphael. Bored, he examined the fire-alarm box; there was little else to do. Fifteen minutes later the system inched Chuck forward one step—like rolling a sequence of ones in Monopoly.

2:05 He waited in the hall for the paperwork to be processed so he could carry it back to the ward. Then he waited on the lawn in front of the building.

2:45 He still waited. The ennui was broken now and then by the staff members and patients who stopped by and chatted for a few minutes on their way to and from appointments.

2:50 Chuck lay in the sun on the lawn.

3:05 Finally, he was informed that he could go back to his ward. The paperwork would follow later.

3:20 Chuck bought a lock at the canteen. His step was bouncy; he moved quickly on the stairs and seemed to enjoy swinging his arms, moving about as if newly freed. This elevation of mood was the result not only of his being back in the hospital. This day was a purposeful one for Chuck. What he was doing was actively changing his life setting. Because the next day would not be so meaningful, the euphoria would wear off quickly.

3:40 Back on his ward, Chuck sat and drank coffee.

EPILOGUE

Chuck's activity level in the hospital during the first two days was a great deal higher than it had been at home. He interacted with a variety of people and seemed less satisfied with sitting and filling time. He was out late drinking with friends on Friday and Saturday nights.

I met with Chuck's parents on Saturday, March 17th. Mrs. Smith said she had cried after Chuck left and that she had felt very depressed. She had been able to unload some of her disappointment by pouring out her troubles to the apartment manager. Then her husband had taken her out for a change of scenery. I reassured them that Chuck was doing well. Jewel asked me to tell Chuck she loved him. She hugged me as I left.

Within months, Chuck had attempted suicide again. This time he took an overdose of medication and locked himself in the trunk of his car. Two days later he regained consciousness, pounded on the inside of the trunk lid, and was released from his erstwhile casket. He voluntarily returned to the hospital.

The next year, Chuck began participation in a V.A. follow-up program. He was given a battery of psychological tests just before his discharge from the hospital. The tests showed him to remain a moderately high suicide risk. On the MMPI test he indicated that his daily life was not full of things that kept him interested, his sex life was unsatisfactory, he felt blue most of the time, he felt sometimes as if he must injure either himself or someone else, there was something wrong with his mind, he was afraid of losing his mind, he worried frequently, he was restless, he had difficulty starting new activities, he was tense and somewhat paranoid, people often disappointed him, he was lonely, life was a strain, he was sensitive, and sometimes he enjoyed hurting persons he loved.

Chuck received outpatient follow-up for six months after his discharge. His physical health remained good, his work and money situation deteriorated; his appearance fluctuated between poor and average. The two variables of self-respect and of love from others fluctuated wildly from month to month.

On March 4, 1977, Dr. Reynolds received a call from Mrs. Smith, who worried that Chuck needed to be rehospitalized. He was resisting her efforts to direct him to the hospital. A clash with his current landlady and a gradually declining ability to function had prompted a crisis from which Chuck had fled, saying he would never allow himself to be taken back to the hospital. Jewel asked if it would be appropriate to have Chuck get in touch with us when she next had contact with him. We encouraged that effort. But no phone call was received.

Subsequently, Chuck was hospitalized, was placed on outpatient status, was hospitalized again, and again was discharged with outpatient follow-up.

REVIEW OF
RELEVANT
LITERATURE

The literature on the schizophrenic and his family is extensive. This review focuses selectively on those aspects most relevant to our area of interest, namely, the problems faced by an identified suicidal patient, diagnosed as schizophrenic, after his release from inpatient treatment in a neuropsychiatric hospital. The major elements in this phase of the life of Chuck Smith are his discharge from the hospital, his reentry into his nuclear family, and his experiences in interacting once more with his family in their setting. All of these elements are embedded in a context of schizophrenia. We believe that Chuck's behavior and the interactions between him and his parents, his sister, and the researcher can best be understood in the context of his schizophrenic family. The suicidal behavior is then seen as one of the symptoms of Chuck's illness, a secondary manifestation of his frustrations.

Our journal observations are made in such a context. To provide a summary background, this report on the literature reviews briefly some of the major theoretical contributions to our understanding of the schizophrenic family, the communication difficulties that characterize such families, and some of the family therapy conducted with schizophrenic families.

THEORIES OF SCHIZOPHRENIA

Buss and Buss (1969) review the major theories about schizophrenia. Five of these, the genetic-neuro, cognitive, motivation, regression, and social isolation theories, are discussed here briefly. The remaining two theories, emphasizing either the role of the family or communication defects, are detailed later. In addition, a theory is reviewed focusing on disturbances in differentiation of the boundaries necessary for a sense of self and an awareness of others in interpersonal relationships.

Genetic-neuro

Meehl (1962) has combined the genetic theory, which assumes schizophrenia to be an inherited biological disposition, and the neuro theory, which assumes a malfunction of the nervous system, into a single theory. A basic assumption is that an inherited defect predisposes the individual to schizophrenia. The defect is assumed to be within the nervous system, specifically in the functioning of the synapses between the neurons. The content of the psychoses is unimportant, inasmuch as this depends on the specific learning that occurs during an individual's life. This learning will vary from person to person, producing different manifestations of the psychosis. The basis of all schizophrenia, however, which is common in every person with such an illness, is the presence of faulty biological processes. The assumption is that these processes are inherited, but the precise mechanism is unknown.

Wender, Rosenthal, Zahn, and Kety (1971) find that the biological parents of children who develop schizophrenia are more disturbed than are the adoptive parents of such children. This suggests to them a strong genetic predisposing factor. They also find, however, that adoptive parents whose children develop schizophrenia are more disturbed than adoptive parents whose children do not develop schizophrenia. This finding suggests that, although there may be environmental predisposing factors, a parental predisposing factor is necessary before the illness will appear.

Cognitive

McGhie and Chapman (1961) characterize the basic problem in schizophrenia as an inability to select, focus on, and regulate incoming information. The schizophrenic becomes confused and inefficient because he is unable to cope with all of the distracting stimuli impinging on him. Faulty processes in attention are the basic contributors to the cognitive dysfunction. The cognitive deficit becomes primary, producing problems in motivation and an overwhelming anxiety, which in turn result in interpersonal and social difficulties.

Motivation

According to Garmezy and Rodnick (1959), the potential schizophrenic has an abnormal sensitivity to criticism which produces excessive anxiety in anticipated and actual interpersonal activities. The schizophrenic's extreme fear of rejection is seen as the basis for his acute discomfort in social activities and as the explanation for his self-imposed isolation from others.

Mednick (1958) assumes that the extreme anxiety found in the schizophrenic interferes with the patient's thinking processes, leading to overgeneralization. The stimuli become more and more frightening, and the person's motivation centers on avoidance. One way to avoid the frightening stimuli is to dwell on remote, irrelevant thoughts and associations. Because the irrelevant associations distract the schizophrenic from the anxiety-producing stimuli, his anxiety level is reduced. As this continues, the reduction of anxiety becomes rewarding and the tendency to think irrelevant and distant thoughts becomes habitual.

Regression

Regression assumes fixed stages in the developmental sequence. The "normal" individual progresses through each stage, mastering the problems in each before proceeding to the next one. Schizophrenic individuals under stress return to behavioral modes characteristic of earlier stages. Kantor and Winder (1959) hypothesize a process-reactive dimension in schizophrenia. They characterize process schizophrenia as the more severe psychosis, with more regression and a greater psychological deficit than is found in reactive schizophrenia. They relate Sullivan's five stages of early childhood to the process-reactive dimension of schizophrenia.

Goldman (1962) assumes that the developmental process moves from an early unorganized and undifferentiated state to a highly organized and differentiated specific state. Differentiation implies the organization of different response modes into varying levels of behaviors. Schizophrenia represents a regression back to the earlier developmental stages, characterized by generalization, diffusion, and lack of differentiation.

Social Isolation

Faris (1934) emphasizes the impact upon an individual of many rejections by fellow members of his community, including his family. This continued rejection and isolation leads to a "shut-in" personality and a turning away from social contacts. The individual no longer checks his notions of reality against social consensus. Instead, he orients his attention more and more toward himself, functioning outside the mainstream of everyday life and gradually drifting into schizophrenia.

None of the above theories contributes much to our understanding of the interaction between Chuck Smith and his family, except perhaps the motivation theory of Garmezy and Rodnick, referring to the schizophrenic's extreme fear of rejection and his drive to avoid criticism. Chuck was uncomfortable in social situations and readily developed a high level of disabling anxiety, most of which he controlled by withdrawal.

Communication

Interest in the communication interactions and their disturbances appeared in the 1950s, but only recently have further studies dealt with this aspect of the problem. Among the earlier investigators, Bateson, Jackson, Haley, and Weakland (1969) developed a theory of schizophrenia based upon that part of communication theory known as the theory of logical types. The central thesis of this theory holds that there is a discontinuity between a class and its members, and that it is never possible for the two to be similar because the term used for a class is at a different level of abstraction. A breakdown occurs in the schizophrenic's ability to discriminate between functioning logical types under certain conditions. The schizophrenic is characteristically weak in receiving messages from other persons, in those he sends out himself, and in referring to his own thoughts, sensations, and percepts. This breakdown usually results from family interactions that lead to unconventional communication habits. The predominant interaction is the "double-bind." Five ingredients are essential to a double-bind. There must be (1) two or more persons,

(2) a repeated experience, (3) a primary negative injunction, (4) a secondary injunction conflicting with the first at an abstract level, and (5) a tertiary negative injunction that prevents the victim from escaping the field.

In the double-bind situation, the individual is involved in an intense relationship in which the other person is expressing two orders of messages, one of which denies the other. The schizophrenic's family situation characteristically consists of a child with a mother who becomes anxious and withdraws if the child responds to her as if she were a loving mother. The possibility of intimate contact with the child arouses intense feelings of anxiety and hostility toward the child. Since these feelings are not acceptable, the mother's problem is to control her anxiety by controlling the closeness between herself and her child. When the child draws too close, the mother feels endangered and responds by beginning to withdraw, but her hostile act produces guilt that she must deny by simulating affection for and closeness with the child. Opposing messages are delivered: (1) a hostile withdrawal and (2) an affectionate closeness. The child is placed in a position where he either cannot or must not accurately interpret her communication if he is to maintain any kind of relationship with her. If he approaches his mother on the basis of his perception of her simulated loving behavior, he provokes in her feelings of fear that force her to withdraw. If the child, in turn, withdraws from her, she interprets the withdrawal as an accusation that she has not been a loving mother. She either punishes him for withdrawing or approaches him to bring him closer. As a result, the child learns either to deny or to distort his communications. He grows up unskilled in communicating, both in his ability to determine what people really mean and in his ability to express what he himself really means. At the same time, the family lacks anyone strong and insightful, such as a father, who can intervene in the relationship between the mother and child and can support the child in the face of the contradictions involved.

Lidz (1973) focuses primarily on family relationships to understand schizophrenia, but he integrates communication disorders into later formulations. He describes the schizophrenic thought disorder as: derailment of associations, deficiency in the ability to categorize, inability to maintain segmental separations, and an egocentric overinclusiveness in the patient's thinking. He builds on Piaget's formulations of cognitive developmental stages—preoperational thinking, concrete thinking, and formal-operational or conceptual thinking—as developing throughout adolescence. All stages require learning of categories and each stage sees continual refinement of them. Everyone must learn his culture's categorical system to be able to think and to communicate coherently. Unless the categorization is learned, expectancies cannot be formed. Without expectancies, intelligent communication is impossible. Lidz feels that the schizophrenic regresses into an intercategorical realm in which he is trying to handle diffusions of himself and his mother along with polymorphous, perverse fantasies that evidence early, regressed, magical thinking.

Because the patients are raised amid irrationality and are exposed to "psychic contagions" within the family which distort and deny the communications, their foundations in reality testing are very tenuous. Even in families in which neither parent can clearly be termed psychotic, irrational developmental settings are found, constructed out of each parent's emotional need to maintain his or her own precarious emotional balance. In part, this explains the strange combination of intrusiveness and imperviousness that characterizes these parents. The parent must be intrusive to control the child better but must at the same time be impervious to the child's own feelings, desires, and needs.

Another confusion found within family communication is "masking." One or both parents may conceal a disturbing situation within the family and may act as if it did not exist, expecting the child similarly to ignore the situation. Lidz relates this to Laing's and Esterson's (1964) concept of "mystification," which describes one person's confusion to the point of insanity in reaction to another person's communication. Wynne and Singer (1963) also comment on the impaired family communication resulting when one or both parents communicate in a blurred, fragmented, or disruptive style, with an inability to focus attention selectively. The pervasive meaninglessness and pointlessness of the communications permits no clear-cut concepts to develop.

King (1975) substantiates the significance of communication disturbance in schizophrenia by examining twelve cases of infantile autism, finding a significantly greater number of double-bind relationships with their mothers among these twelve than among matched controls. Reiss (1976) also confirms the causal rather than the epiphenomenal role played by communication disturbances in the pathogenesis of schizophrenia. Communication processes in the family are seen as significant in the child's development of attentional and perceptual capacities. Feldman (1975) extends the concept of the double-bind beyond its original sociological, interpersonal bounds, hypothesizing that the double-bind also becomes intra-psychic, produced by the schizophrenic within himself. This further destroys his ability to categorize and to conceptualize, producing immobilization reactions and inappropriate responses to culturally recognized stimuli.

Frank, Allen, Sleen, and Myers (1976), study the language patterns of schizophrenic mothers and their young children, comparing them with the speech patterns in normal mothers of normal children and in normal mothers of autistic children. The schizophrenic mothers are found to produce more deficient or distorted language in their interactions with their children, while the children show lags in language development and distortions that are often similar to those found in the autistic children. Clark and Cullen (1974, 1975) compare the amount of conflicting communication in schizophrenics' and normals' families and friends and find a significant association between the number of conflicting associations and schizophrenia. Winter (1975) finds marked similarities in the way parents and their schizophrenic children construe events, ideas, and constructs.

The communication theory of schizophrenia is highly pertinent to our understanding of the Smith family. They have developed many special forms of communicating, unique for each family member, and the numerous double-binds witnessed in the period of observation indicates that this mechanism has played a significant role in Chuck's life. Intrusiveness and imperviousness also predominate in the relationship between Chuck and his mother.

Family

The role of the family in schizophrenia has received the most intensive scrutiny by researchers over the past few decades, not only in terms of its genetic contributions but also in terms of the communication patterns it establishes and the interactional patterns it develops between parents and between parents and children. A number of early studies noted pathological relationships between the mothers and their schizophrenic children (Prout and White, 1950; Mark, 1953; Freeman and Grayson, 1955; Rodnick and Garmezy, 1957). Frieda Fromm-Reichman introduced the term "schizo-phrenogenic mother" as early as 1939, describing her character structure within a psychoanalytic framework. Gerard and Siegel (1950) found the parents of schizophrenic patients to be immature and inadequate and to have extreme reaction formations. The schizophrenic child always seemed to be the focal point of distorted relationships within the family.

Clausen and Kohn

Clausen and Kohn (1960) feel that parental pathology can support equally well a genetic or a psychogenic explanation of the schizophrenic. Probably the best interpretation is that of interaction between genetic susceptibility and the social matrix within which the child attempts to achieve his identity. The authors concentrate on the social matrix, hypothesizing that families produce schizophrenics out of the pathology of the parents. When the marital relationship fails to produce satisfaction, the child becomes more and more the mother's source of satisfaction and the basis for her existence. This produces an increasing need for control over the child, so that she becomes both the source of and the authority for his affection. As the child attempts to establish his independence, behaving in ways that oppose her wishes or moral standards, she is likely to react both with anxiety and with feelings of aggression. The mother is then caught in a quandary, for to deny the moral imperatives of mother love is to deny her claim of worth. Instead, unacceptable impulses are denied while stereotyped mother-role norms are verbalized. If the father is at all assertive, conflicts arise with the mother over her preoccupation with the child and her efforts at overcontrol. If the father is a very passive figure, the battle is generally resolved in the form of a continuing tight but stressful bond between the mother and child.

Alanen

The Finnish researcher, Alanen (1958), focused mainly on the relationship between the mother and her schizophrenic child(ren) by comparing 100 unselected schizophrenic patients and their mothers with 20 neurotic patients and their mothers, and with 20 "normal" persons and their mothers. Among the mothers of the schizophrenics, he found that the mothers themselves had had disturbed childhoods, providing a foundation for disturbance in their schizophrenic children. The mothers were marked by embittered aggressiveness toward their own childhood experiences, especially toward their own mothers. Bitterness toward their fathers was far less general. The mothers' poor relationships with their own mothers seems to have been an essential factor, contributing to the weaknesses of their egos and to the generation of schizoid traits. More than half the mothers were suffering from personality disorders that were classified as near-psychotic and schizoid.

The parents' marriages were generally disturbed, characterized by pathological jealousy and infantile behavior. The predominant theme was a badly disturbed, frustrated woman marrying a disturbed man, resulting in a marriage that led to further frustration and aggressiveness. There was constant mutual hostility accompanying stronger than ordinary dependence of the spouses on each other which induced them, despite everything, to continue their lives together. The atmosphere was one of irrational demands complicated by serious disagreement and conflict between the parents.

The characteristic attitude of the mother toward her schizophrenic child verged on complete domination, with little or no understanding of the child's needs or feelings. Her overwhelming possessiveness suppressed the child's development into an independent person and at the same time bound him to an unempathic authority. This attitude had its roots in an anxious, ambivalent hostility felt by the mother toward her child. Her loveless, aggressive attitude distorted the child's development through the early, important years of his life. He lived surrounded by demands that he was forced to attempt to meet as a condition for love. The emotional tone of the mother's dominance differed depending on whether the patient was male or female. The mothers of male patients were more often possessively protective whereas the mothers of female patients were more often aggressively hostile and at the same time suppressively protective.

Bowen

Murray Bowen (1960) has observed entire families while they lived for varying periods of time in a laboratory environment. His most significant finding is the evidence of different emotional patterns of dysfunctioning between the parents. Both parents are equally immature, but one denies the immaturity, operating with a facade of overadequacy, while the other emphasizes the immaturity, presenting a facade of inadequacy. When the mother functions as overadequate, she appears dominating and aggressive and the father appears helpless. When the roles are reversed, the father appears authoritative and cruel while the mother appears ineffectual and whining. Considerable anger is present because the overadequate member sees self as being forced to take responsibility, resenting the other as a shirker. The inadequate parent sees self as being forced to submit and the other as dominating.

The mother-child relationship becomes the most intense relationship in the families, with the mother usually more invested in the child than in the husband. The mother frequently overcompensates for her own immaturity by overinvesting in the helpless child. The mother makes two demands of the child: that the child remain helpless and that the child become a gifted person. The father remains emotionally divorced from the mother but tries to develop a closer relationship with the child. This is very difficult, however, until he has first been able to modify his emotional divorce from the mother. The research families operated on a peace-at-any-price principle, with the child automatically doing things that ensured a less anxious and a more predictable mother.

The problem for the schizophrenic patient is much greater than that of the "normal" adolescent, who is able to expect help from parents while he is growing up and is then capable of making a start outside the family. In the schizophrenic family dilemma, before he can begin to resolve the problems of a "normal" adolescent, the child has to deal not only with the mother's efforts to hold him back but with his own impulses to return to her. While in the home, the patient uses denial and isolation to escape the mother's prevailing influence. The psychosis represents an unsuccessful attempt to adapt within the severe psychological impairment to the demands of adult functioning.

In the treatment process, the most striking observation is that if the parents are able to develop an emotional closeness so that they are more involved with each other than they are with the patient, the patient improves. When either parent, however, becomes more invested in the patient than in the other parent, the regression is almost immediate and automatic. Under the condition of "emotional divorce," any type of "management approach" is equally unsuccessful.

Lidz and Associates

Some of the most extensive work in studying schizophrenic families has been conducted by Lidz and his associates at Yale (1957, 1965, 1973). Their early studies concentrate on the schizophrenic family and those interactions between members which seem most pertinent to the development of the illness in the child. The role of the father in the pathology of the family is emphasized. In later writings, disturbances within communication are recognized as highly significant and are integrated into their hypotheses about the development of schizophrenic functioning. Their dynamic theory of personality development includes analysis of the central functions of the family in guiding the integration of its children, and of the significance of language in human adaptation and functioning, including the various stages of cognitive development as they are correlated with the stages of personality development. Language and ego-functioning are seen as operating hand in hand, so that distortions of language and reasoning can lead to gross disturbances in behavior.

The authors presume that a family, or some carefully planned substitute, is a basic requirement for the development of a human being. It is necessary not only for his protection and nurturance during the long years of his immaturity but also for his development into an integrated individual who possesses the techniques, knowledge, and roles required for survival and adaptation. The family has the tasks of structuring the child's personality and of carrying out his basic socialization and acculturation. The families of schizophrenic patients fail in these responsibilities by not providing one or more of the four basic family functions: nurturance, a dynamic family organization, integration into the social system, and transmission of the basic elements of the culture, particularly language, with its pertinent system of meanings and logic.

Two main types of depriving family settings have been described within the schizophrenic family; namely, the skewed and the schismatic. One or both of the parents in these families are generally profoundly disturbed themselves and extend these disturbances into the functioning of the family and the development of any children. In the skewed family, the disturbed parent is most often the mother whose egocentricity is not countered by her spouse. The mother does not establish boundaries between herself and the child and instead uses the child to complete her life, remaining extremely intrusive throughout the child's life into adolescence and adulthood. She is generally impervious to the needs of the child or of other family members as separate individuals. At the same time, the father provides a very poor model inasmuch as he is unable to counter the mother's methods in rearing the child. The child grows up believing that he cannot get along with his mother and that she cannot get along without him. He has mixed and ambivalent feelings, fearing engulfment by her and needing to escape the overly protective involvement, but experiencing any movement toward separation as synonymous with killing her. The father is unable to assume an active role in the family, provides a poor model for his son, and frequently is highly disturbed himself. Basically, the mother is unable to realize that other family members can perceive and feel differently from her and that their lives are not merely complements of hers.

The schismatic family is characterized by much more open conflict between the spouses, with each undercutting the other and competing for the loyalty of their children. Because the husbands are markedly insecure, they need to have constant admiration and to derogate the position and value of the wife and mother. Although both mothers and fathers are frequently extremely disturbed, the father may be able to function well outside of the family. Because she is so poorly developed herself, the mother is unable to provide the children with a feeling of meaning and a sense of individuality.

The child in such families is caught in a bind, because trying to please either parent provokes rebuff and rejection by the other. Sometimes there is an indirect attempt to salvage the parents' marriage by accepting the role of family scapegoat. In such instances, the child begins to behave in ways that seem causal of the parental strife, masking the incompatibility of the parents. But the child pays the price of failing to invest in his own developmental needs.

Lidz and his associates emphasize the significance of the father in the families of schizophrenics. They identify five prominent, overlapping patterns among these fathers: (1) fathers of female patients who are in constant conflict with their wives, with most of the hostility focused on the wife; (2) fathers of some male patients who direct their hostility toward the offspring rather than the wife; (3) fathers who have exaggerated concepts of themselves that verge on features of paranoid grandiosity (such fathers are aloof from their children and demand adulation from the mothers); (4) fathers who have failed in life and have become virtual nonentities in the home; and (5) fathers who are very passive and act the part of siblings in the family, accepting their wives as the grown-up authorities.

Lidz describes egocentric overinclusiveness as the schizophrenic patient's tendency to believe that he is the focal point of events that in actuality are fortuitous to his life. He also tends to distort reality to his own needs as he regresses to preoperational thinking and a belief in the omnipotence of thought. Overt psychosis does not always follow a traumatic occurrence. Very often nothing traumatic has occurred and, rather, the patient has simply failed to progress beyond a crucial developmental phase. Such a phase is the result of the many deficiencies and distortions in the developmental settings that the schizophrenic has endured.

Wynne and Associates

Wynne and his associates (1958, 1963) have derived the concept of a "pseudomutuality" from the construct of mutuality which, in turn, is based on maintaining a sense of relation between one's own behavior and expectations and the behavior and expectations of other person(s). Pseudomutuality is characterized by a strong need to fit personalities together at the expense of differentiating between the identities of the persons in the relationship. This contrasts with genuine mutuality, with its mutual recognition of each individual's potentiality and capacities. In pseudomutuality, divergence is perceived as leading to a disruption of the relationship and so is to be avoided at all costs. Old expectations and roles, even though outgrown and inappropriate, continue to structure the interaction and thus to constrict growth and to impoverish interpersonal experiences. Pseudomutuality in itself does not necessarily produce schizophrenia, but it is assumed to be a major feature of the setting in which schizophrenia develops when other factors are also present.

In the schizophrenic family, there is a fixed organization of a limited number of engulfing roles. This role interaction is not changed, regardless of new situations. As a result, there is an absence of spontaneity, novelty, humor, or zest in the participation together. Any events that might lead to deviations within the family role structure are excluded from recognition or are delusionally interpreted. This prevents the development of a meaning to the events by which the individual family member might be able to differentiate his personal identity either inside or outside of the family role structure. Instead, the roles become diffused, blurred, and distorted. The family role structure is therefore all-encompassing, with the family members acting as a completely self-sufficient social system within a completely encircling boundary. This elastic boundary stretches to include desirable events and contracts to exclude events that are interpreted as undesirable.

The family maintains a subculture of myths, legends, and ideologies which emphasizes the danger of divergence from the fixed family role structure. The family may at times develop legends about illness and violence which serve as continuous reminders of the consequence of divergence. Sometimes the anxiety over divergency may lead to a contradictory disapproval of the same behavior that had previously been approved. This contradiction itself, however blatant, is often blandly ignored.

Each family member is expected to conceal large areas of his experience from the others. At the same time the secrecy may be contradicted by an insistence that family members investigate what they have been declaring to be private. Sometimes there is a tendency to formalize experiences, such as scheduling discussions within the family on impersonal subjects. Actually, these serve primarily to limit the areas for arguments. Also, another common operation is the use of intermediaries between family members. In such instances, instructions are administered through a chain of intermediaries so that the demand is not experienced as coming from a family member.

The schizophrenic member of the family may be labeled as the scapegoat and all of the blame may then be localized in him. (Bell and Vogel introduced this concept in 1960.) Everyone in the family becomes anxious if there is any attempt to disturb this role structure. The ostracized person plays an important covert family role in maintaining the pseudomutuality of the rest of the family.

The fragmentation of experience, the identity, the diffusion, and the disturbed modes of perception in communication all contribute to a marked constriction and impoverishment in ego-functioning and development, leaving the potential schizophrenic particularly unprepared in those ego skills and perceptions that make possible the assumption of adult roles. As a result, the schizophrenic develops not only an active investment in maintaining the equilibrium of the family patterns but an immense skill in fulfilling the family complementarity, which saves the family as well as himself from dissolution.

Acute schizophrenic panic and disorganization represent an identity crisis resulting from some movement within the family role structure. Sometimes the psychotic episode represents a failed attempt at obtaining individuation; sometimes independence is achieved by withdrawal, which then serves the purpose of allowing the family to reestablish a modified structure for itself. The acute schizophrenic episode represents the breakdown of pseudomutuality, its attempted restoration, the attainment of a distorted kind of individuation, and a vicarious expression of the need in other family members for individuation. "The chronic state that follows can then be regarded as the return to pseudomutuality at a greater distance, with symptoms that represent a more stable compromise between an expression of individuation and a failure at individuation, between acceptance of a particular family role and nonacceptance, between achievement of relation and disruption of relation" (1958:220).

Blatt and Wild

Blatt and Wild (1976) have extended the work of Lidz by focusing on the concept of boundaries between self and others. One of the most basic steps in human development is the evolution of a capacity to separate objects. In schizophrenia, this inability to differentiate, articulate, and represent boundaries is seen as evidence of those profound disturbances in the sense of self and interpersonal relationships which characterize the illness.

Differentiation is assumed to develop gradually. In the initial phase, people and the mother are not seen as objects separate from and external to the infant. In the next phase, a symbiotic phase of development, there is some awareness of self and mother as separate, but there are at the same time strong tendencies toward experiences of fusion and attempts to minimize any differentiation between self and nonself. The third phase is conceptualized as the capacity to perceive boundaries between self and the external world, between self and other people, and between self and human, animate, and inanimate objects. Separation is perceived between an object and its representation as well as between self and nonself and between internal experience and external objects and events.

The authors do not assume that boundary disturbances are always present in all schizophrenias. They do assume that one fundamental dimension in schizophrenia is an instability in the concept of the object, and that there is a particular vulnerability to situations, such as intense interpersonal interactions, that stimulate fears of rejection and abandonment and may threaten a tentative concept of the object. Schizophrenics show difficulty in establishing focus, attention, and task set. These difficulties have been interpreted as reflecting a lack of inhibition of irrelevant stimuli leading to distractibility, passive assimilation of stimuli, diffuse and global experiencing, and inability to pursue a task consistently. Language disturbances in schizophrenia have been seen as deriving from an inability to maintain boundary distinctions between objects and their symbolic referents.

From observations of their reactions to the Rorschach, Blatt and Wild find that figure and ground perception differentiates between kinds of schizophrenic patients. Chronic and undifferentiated schizophrenics have difficulty in articulating figure from ground, with much greater tendency toward perceptual fusion. Paranoid and acute schizophrenic patients, however, appear to have greater than average field articulation and less tendency toward perceptual fusion. The degree of boundary disturbance in individual parents, the family patterns of role relationships, and the overall family styles of communication contribute both to the etiology and to the maintenance of schizophrenic difficulties in differentiating self from family and establishing an independent existence.

The schizophrenic is caught in a "need-fear dilemma," in which he seeks both fusion and separation. But he is unable to tolerate either, because both feel as if they are annihilation. Parents of schizophrenics often have boundary disturbances of their own. Interaction and communication within the family contribute to the maintenance of the schizophrenic patient's difficulty in establishing himself as an independent person.

Rogler and Hollingshead

Rogler and Hollingshead (1965) have examined 40 schizophrenic families in the San Juan area of Puerto Rico. The spouses are between 20 and 39 years of age, and the families are in the lowest socioeconomic stratum, residing in the slums of San Juan. These families are compared with a corresponding group of nonschizophrenic families from the survey sample. The parents are generally illiterate, the fathers are predominantly agricultural laborers, and the mothers are employed mostly in the home. The families are large and all are poor. Mental illness is found in half of the families of orientation. Comparison with the parental families of persons who are mentally healthy, however, indicates no significant differences socially or culturally. There are equivalent economic deprivations and physical illnesses, and there are basic similarities in social life, number of friends, and amount of leisure time.

The authors conclude that, in many ways, the Puerto Rican culture contributes to the mental illness. In this culture, for example, a set of crises appear at marriage. The girl must adapt to a change in her role and in all of the mores and activities she has been taught. A sharp discontinuity occurs in social conditioning. The male encounters a strain between being a good husband and being the all-conquering "macho," which he was before marriage.

A complex of mounting, interrelated crises typically becomes manifest during the twelve months before the onset of the illness. These include increasing economic difficulties, physical problems, interspouse conflicts, and difficulties with members of the extended family. Schizophrenic men experience particular difficulty in their work and with their associates on the job, and they are confronted with a loss of employment earnings as they are forced to stay away from work for increasingly longer periods of time. The women experience mounting difficulty in establishing meaningful relations with other persons.

As sociologists, Rogler and Hollingshead find relatively few clues in childhood and adolescent experiences for understanding the way the illness develops. Instead, they attribute basic causality to recent events, that is, to the emergence of a set of insoluble, mutually reinforcing problems that entrap the person. Within the families, differences are based on whether the sick person is male or female. The families of the male schizophrenic are more closely linked to the wife's relatives than to the husband's because the wife turns to her own family for help. When the wife is schizophrenic, the relationship between the nuclear and the extended family becomes fragmented. When the husband is sick, the woman takes over to nurture and protect the male. She becomes dominant in the family and work roles becomes reversed. The sick male becomes extremely dependent upon the extended family. His role is at marked variance with the

cultural definition of macho, which emphasizes masculine independence and freedom. When the wife is sick, tension points are exacer-
bated and the family is disorganized. For the sick woman, the role
becomes inconsistent with feminine behavior because it includes
rebellion against husband and other authoritative figures. The woman
is deeply integrated into the extended family inasmuch as her whole
social space and horizons are encompassed by the family system of
which she is a member. Discord and confusion envelop the children
more often when the wife or mother is the sick one.

When the husband is sick, the healthy wife must not only cope
with the loss of the breadwinner but also with a husband who is
nervous, fatigued, and withdrawn. This takes a toll on the wife, as is
indicated by the fact that the rate of physical illness for the wife
doubles from the first five years to the second five years after the
husband's mental illness occurs. The husband's decompensation into
schizophrenia creates multiple problems involving subsistence,
health, and interpersonal relations. When the wife is disabled, an
array of disturbing symptoms is projected onto the nuclear and the
extended family. The marriage tends to fall apart, the children are
trapped in a disorganized family milieu, and the extended family is
fragmented. All of this reaffirms the functional importance of the
woman's role in preserving the inner coherence of the family.

Mishler and Waxler

An interesting study by Mishler and Waxler (1968) compared 32
schizophrenic families with 17 normal families in terms of qualities
of interaction. Their study design required two family interviews
with two different siblings. All of the schizophrenics were first
divided by sex and then were classified as having a good or a poor
premorbid social adjustment by the score obtained on the Phillips
Scale of Premorbid Adjustment. This scale rates the patient's past
social history for recent sexual adjustment, for social aspects of
sexual life during adolescence, for social aspects of recent sexual life,
for history of personal relations, and for recent adjustment in personal relations. Families were interviewed by means of the Revealed-
Differences Technique, which asks parents and child to develop a
response to a particular situation. An observer recorded all of the
information about the discussion from behind a one-way mirror,

categorizing the observations in terms of expressiveness, strategy of attention, strategy of person control, speech disruption, and responsiveness.

Many of the results were consistent with observations of earlier researchers. For example, "normal" families were both more expressive and more positive in the quality of their expressed affect. Good premorbid families tended to be more instrumental in their behavior and relatively negative in the quality of their expressed affect.

In terms of direction of expressed affect, "normal" families were consistently low and poor premorbid families were consistently high. This was interpreted to mean that members of "normal" families could direct their affect toward a variety of targets other than those immediately present in the situation and that they were consistent in both direct and indirect expressions. In contrast, the degree to which the poor premorbid families focused their affect on persons present indicated a more concrete and particularistic mode of expression. In the families of males, good premorbids tended to be low. This was interpreted to indicate their unwillingness to risk direct confrontation with others. Lidz (1973) also found that male patients came from skewed families in which patterns of conflict and hostility were less manifest, and that female schizophrenics came from schismatic families in which the conflict among the members was more open.

In terms of control strategies, the patient and his mother in the male patient families took relatively high power positions and tended to defer to each other. The father exerted little influence on the family. In female patient families, little attention was accorded the daughter. The mother and daughter did not try to influence the proceedings, although the mother in these latter families appeared to be more generally powerful than the father. In none of the patients' families were there suitable parental models for identification for either sons or daughters. The schizophrenic son was allied with his mother against a weak father, and the isolated and powerless schizophrenic daughter had to contend with a powerful mother.

In the area of speech disruption, good premorbid families were found to be most orderly and well controlled in their speech. This was interpreted to mean that speech became an almost ritualistic language, providing neither new information to the listener nor permitting the possibility of change.

In the area of responsiveness, poor premorbid families were most different from the "normals" in that they focused their attention on the rules of the experimental situation. They behaved as if they were somewhat confused and as if they were trying to discover a rule that would tell them what to do. The good premorbids showed a pattern of controlled and rigid response with a tendency to conduct their relations with each other in a somewhat impersonal and abstract way.

One of the major findings in the study was that generalized family styles of interaction expressed in behavior appeared to be stronger than intrafamilial role differentials. The authors attribute this to a "strain toward consistency" within a family which produces similarity to society and community styles of interaction.

Other Researchers

Lerner's (1969) investigation of the way schizophrenic families resolve conflict within their own group also uses the Revealed-Differences Technique. He finds consistent differences between the processes used by the schizophrenic families and "normal" controls, with the former exhibiting behavior described as pseudomutual by Wynne, Rykoff, Day, and Hirsch (1958). Lerner finds that the use by the family of distortion and masking varies proportionally with the premorbid level of social maturity and severity of thought disturbance in the child.

Schizophrenic family interaction is shown in sharp relief in a study by Suzuki (1972) using the consensus Rorschach. Twelve schizophrenic families and twelve "normal" control families were administered both individual and consensus Rorschachs, and their behaviors and attitudes during testing were observed. Suzuki concludes that, although many of the responses of the schizophrenic group were in consensus form, they were not actual group responses. Usually the opinions of the parents were used but the others were ignored. The parents would force a response from their children and then would ignore or deny it. The parents were also unable to decide anything without mutual agreement, whether they were highly dependent on each other or were antagonistic and mistrustful.

Support for Lidz's formulations about schizophrenic family patterns is found in a study by Takatomi, Suzuki, and Dendo (1972), who differentiate two types of patients based on syndromes and family relationships through an analysis of the family consensus Rorschachs of six male and six female schizophrenics. Type I patients have typical neurotic symptoms, and Type II patients have more typical psychotic symptoms. Type I female patients are rejected by their mothers with mutual dislike. This female patient comes to rely upon her father, but the father's incompetency leads to frustration. Type I male patients are unable to rebel against the authoritative attitudes of their fathers because of the lack of support from their mothers. Type I parents are like Lidz's skewed families, showing noncomplementary dependency without great disharmony. Type II parents ignore their children, especially female children. Male children are tied to their mothers in a double-bind relationship.

Waring (1978) is highly critical of present-day researchers into schizophrenia who have continued to use uncritically the concepts introduced by early investigators, despite the fact that many of the latter have moved ahead to new concepts. Among such concepts Waring would include: the schizophrenogenic mother, schism and skew, pseudomutuality, double-binds, and mystification. He feels that only Bowen's theory of "emotional divorce" has received any empirical support. There is also little evidence that these phenomena are specific to families of schizophrenics. Experimental evidence supports the following findings, but only in terms of providing correlations and not in terms of being necessary or sufficient for the development of schizophrenia: (1) more parents of schizophrenics are psychiatrically disturbed than are parents of "normal" children, and more of the mothers are "schizoid"; (2) mothers of schizophrenics show more concern and protectiveness than mothers of "normal" children, both in the current situation and in their attitudes to the children before they fell ill; (3) the preschizophrenic child more frequently manifests physical ill health or mild disability early in life than the "normal" child; (4) the parents of schizophrenics show more conflict and disharmony than do the parents of other psychiatric patients; (5) the work of Wynne and Singer strongly suggests that parents of schizophrenics communicate abnormally, but their concept of pseudomutuality has not been tested; and (6) schizophrenics involved in tense relationships with their relatives or spouses are more likely to relapse than those whose relationships are less tense.

The theories relating schizophrenia to the family seem to strike the most responsive chord in relation to our understanding of the Smith family development. The concepts of Alanen, Bowen, Lidz, and Wynne appear most relevant, especially Lidz's formulation of the skewed family, in which the egocentricity of the mother is not countered by the spouse, who serves as a poor role model. Wynne's description of pseudomutuality fits the Smith family, which expands and contracts to accommodate its deviant member, Chuck, but which never allows the individuation and independence that would permit Chuck to become his own person. Family complementarity is maintained at the expense of the individual. Some members of the family escape, but the mutual dependence between family and Chuck is too deeply entrenched to be broken.

TREATMENT

The family is considered to play a primary role in the treatment of the schizophrenic patient (Beels, 1975). Friedman (1962) notes a major advantage in that the family becomes a captive patient and must deal with its problem. The family unit cannot simply exclude the problem by sending the patient to the hospital, and the domestic emotional climate cannot so readily obscure unverbalized problems behind a facade of family adjustment. Realities underlying family myths are also clarified. On a practical basis, the family is the most important community resource for the schizophrenic when he is released from the hospital. As Evans and Bullard (1960) point out, the family provides financial security, available living space, and a willingness and capacity to support the sick family member. These are key elements in the readjustment of the patient back into the community.

An extensive study of the impact of family psychotherapy has been carried out by Friedman and his associates (1965). They detail intensive therapies with families of schizophrenics, offering conclusions about the most appropriate model for understanding the illness and the family context in which it was developed. Their working hypothesis perceives the nuclear family as a social system, with important structural triads, embedded in a larger social system. In addition, the family social system is viewed as a very dynamic organism that is never in a static condition, in which equilibrium refers to the family stability. In turn, stability is dependent upon differentiation in the present and future roles in the family environment.

The therapists suggest that within the family no single factor, such as a faulty mother-infant relationship, seems likely to cause schizophrenia by itself. Rather, the structure, milieu, and interaction of the family are somehow detrimental to the ego development and social adjustment of the children. Schizophrenia appears to arise from an intense pathological family relationship rather than from neglect or from the absence of a relationship. In addition to genetic factors, there seem to be at least five characteristics attributable to schizophrenic families: (1) excessively closed family systems, (2) shared family myths or delusions, (3) paralogic modes of thinking in all the family members, (4) lack of individuation and self-identity of members from the family "ego mass" (Bowen, 1960), and (5) intense, pathological, symbiotic attachments of the child to parents and of parents to grandparents.

The interpersonal relationships in families seem typically to be split and compartmentalized, being characterized by stereotypical, static, and symbiotic dyads rather than by flexible triadic or four-person functioning units. As in reports by other researchers, the family organization of the schizophrenic can be variously characterized as rigidly stable, as excessively impervious to external environments, as controlling and distorting the interaction of family members with outer environments, and as distorting the usual culturally defined role expectancies within the family while maintaining superficial conformity to external standards. The family also suffers from overcontrol and suppression of affect, from massive denial and shallowness of affect appropriate to the situation, and from vagueness, blurring, and fragmentation in the family communication. It is an organization where the members often do not hear each other or reach each other.

Friedman and associates (1965) suggest that the core difficulty in the marital relationship is extreme marital schism, with associated mutual distrust and derogation, masking of disagreement and conflict, and a resolution into "pseudomutuality." Most of the families studied are extremely isolated with little intermingling and contact either with relatives or with friends outside the family. Patterns of living are rigid and fixed instead of flexible and modifiable. The purpose of the family seems to be to maintain the status quo of the family living pattern.

Trouble arises within the disturbed families when any member attempts to diverge or to initiate a new direction. The response is generally not to the proposed issue. It is in reaction to the family member who suggests change. Active psychosis in the child is seen as a protection for the rest of the family from overt psychotic manifestations. Although there are evidences of psychotic degrees of denial and paranoid projection in many of the parents, they are nevertheless able to maintain an adequate degree of social and vocational functioning so long as the child is actively regressed and symptomatic. Most often there is an intense pathological symbiosis between the mother and the schizophrenic child. The father, however, is an important contributory factor in maintaining and furthering the schizophrenic process. He achieves this by passive ineffectual abdication of his role as husband and father, or by aiding and abetting the symbiosis, or by engaging in splits and alliances and even by taking over the pathological mothering role.

Friedman and associates (1965) describe the reaction of the family system to the intervention of therapeutic agents as occurring in one of two pathological ways: by mobilizing its defenses to keep the therapist on the periphery, or by permitting the therapist to invade the sanctity of the inner boundary of its feelings and sentiments and then by swallowing up the therapist and incorporating him into their pathological system without changing it. At the same time, the family as a functionally helpless organism attaches itself to the therapist.

Umbarger and Hare (1973) have found that when the parents draw closer as a marital couple, they increase their tolerance for an independent life for their schizophrenic son. They strongly urge drawing firm generational lines in the family treatment of a schizophrenic in that this helps family members to disengage from each other and increases the possibility of focusing on essential themes.

Waring (1978), despite his criticisms of previous work with families of schizophrenics, feels that evaluative research on the effectiveness of family therapy with families of schizophrenics is now possible. Terms used before can now be operationally defined and reliably measured. Methodologies for appropriate sampling and matching for controls are available and the testing of hypotheses is feasible. Such evaluative research will be necessary, the author feels, before "family therapy can become more than a highly fascinating and experimental technique in the total management of schizophrenic patients" (1978:56).

V
ANALYSIS
AND DISCUSSION

Just as shared, learned, and repeated patterns of behavior exist among larger groups of people, so do such behavior patterns occur within family units. This patterned behavior with its inferred cognitive and emotional concomitants is called "family culture." Some elements of any family's culture are shared by many other families in the larger sociocultural system. Such elements as interactional dominance of the male as "household head," or the valuing of "togetherness" in the family, or the emphasis on sustained effortful work as a means to worthwhile goals may be common to numerous families in a given society.

Nonetheless, every family possesses unique elements of family culture, shared by very few families or by no other family in that society. This study has aimed at describing the family culture of a single family unit. The family selected for study was special in the sense that one of its members was suicidal.

Suicidal behavior, like most behavior, appears to be learned. But the learning is not simple; it involves the development of complex short-term plans and long-term life strategies. Much of this learning takes place within the network of family reinforcements and understandings, that is, within the "family culture." The research approach employed in this study was to look within the family culture for patterned behaviors that seemed to influence the development of suicidal activities by stimulating or retarding them in various ways.

We have presented a chronological account of the Smith family's interactions, particularly those directly affecting Chuck Smith's life. Our analysis of that material begins by focusing on some of the interactional themes exhibited by family members. Our initial detailing of Jewel's patterns of domination and negativism, and her tactics for control of others, is followed by an examination of various family responses to these patterns.

JEWEL'S DOMINATION

"After breakfast you can start putting the laundry in the car."

"You didn't empty your ashtray."

She rises to adjust the television picture.

"Donna would be that way too if I let her."

She offers directions from the back seat of the car.

"Aren't you beginning to get a little cool, David?" I shut the door.

"Move over." Chuck ignored her. Jewel sat on him.

"Turn the light on please." "Why?" " 'Cause I *want* it on."

"Don't talk too long on the phone."

As we left Jewel told us dessert would be served at 8:30. She could serve it any time but she wanted us back by then.

Jewel told me her version of what led to her husband's giving up alcohol. She told him, "I know you've got the ability. Now do it or else!" And he "straightened up."

"Aren't you going to study today?"

"Leon, your voice is too loud."

Jewel tried to direct the way Chuck was taking out the trash. He told her *he* was doing it. "Here you're a grown man, and Mama still treats you like a little boy. Someday I'll get over it. Won't you be glad when I do?" Chuck's reply, "It doesn't matter."

There was no major area of Chuck's life that she knew about over which Jewel failed to try to exert control. She woke him directly or by puttering about noisily when she felt it was time for him to get up. She engaged him in conversation or busied herself about the couch when she considered him to be napping too frequently. She moved him into the bedroom one afternoon so he could "rest better." As for eating, Jewel tried to determine the time, the amount, and the variety of her family's meals. One afternoon, she told me she would hold lunch until Chuck awoke. Then she went ahead, prepared it anyway, and wakened him. She would enforce or sabotage her children's diets, depending on her mood.

She tried to direct Chuck's study time, where he studied, and what lamp he used. She offered directive opinions about friends, driving routes, and television programs. She provided words when Chuck paused in midsentence. Within a few minutes, she reminded him twice to rinse out the tub after his shower. For a considerable time after his discharge, Jewel controlled Chuck's access to the apartment by lending him her keys when he went out and specifying when she needed them back. She dominated conversations, storytelling, family get-togethers, her grandchildren, virtually every area that allowed some exertion of strong influence. Had it been possible, she would have liked to control as well Chuck's drinking, his schizophrenia, and his suicidality. We shall have more to say about the cost to Chuck of retaining his autonomy in those areas.

Jewel's pattern was to stack control on control by setting up and then negating or preventing another's behavior, as when she arranged to have Chuck take her to the hardware store, then would not let him do so. Or "Go get my (newspaper). You don't have to go right now."

The reverse side of her dominance was her resistance to outside control over her own life. She hated to be tied down to routines and schedules. Taking medication *as directed* was an onerous burden, partly circumvented by taking the pills fifteen minutes early each time so she would not forget. On trips, she did not like scheduled tours. When Mr. Smith told her not to put her coffee cup on the arm of the sofa, she flared up at his directiveness, challenged him, and did as she pleased. Similarly, when Chuck told her to wake him for dessert she replied, "I will not," and she didn't.

Because Jewel's critical stance was pervasive, it was easy to document. On March 13th, for example, she sat smoking in a chair after doing dishes. Her talk was of Miss France (a snob), Lou Rawls (a phony), Tony Bennett (ugly), and a star (Jewel had forgotten her name) who turned Jewel's stomach and was not accepted by the public. Furthermore, she did not like "Laugh In" or "Hee Haw"; the show she had liked, "Mission Impossible," had gone off the air. Finally, Jack Webb played stereotyped roles, had lost his spark, was about to hit rock bottom, and would lose his shirt.

The air smelled bad to Mrs. Smith; food odors, smoke, even her own hair contributed to the staleness. Sickness, too, was all around: the cancer of a friend, a dying acquaintance. "Bad, bad, bad," she sighed. The rooms in the apartment were dark and dismal; her carpet, couch, and chair were "drab" and "depressing." Her world was filled with people who acted in thoughtlessly harmful ways without realizing what they were doing. Other tenants were rude, nursing-home residents were tragic victims, owners were greedy, executives were winos.

The sting of the critical negativism was blunted sometimes by humor, as when Jewel laughed while criticizing her husband for blowing wax over the table when he blew the candles out. But when the laughter ceased, the sting of that criticism, like all the others, persisted.

Jewel recognized her sensitivity to the negative side of life. But she considered her pessimism to be balanced equally by an appreciation of life's brighter aspects. Perhaps this appreciation was of herself. Although she found the world deserving of much criticism, her references to herself were primarily praise-filled. She spoke favorably of her own handicraft products. She described herself as clairvoyant, bright, and aware of what was going on around her. She bragged about her skill at hunting, driving, and swinging from a rope. She spoke with pride of her pomegranate jelly, her success in previous jobs, her ability to make an old dress look good, and her "superhearing" capacity.

Jewel reeled off to Chuck a series of tragedies that had happened recently to people in the nursing home she used to manage. She said, "They seem to think that if I'd been there, these things wouldn't have happened—but they would."

Jewel talked of Aunt Mildred. She couched her monologue as usual in terms of praise of self and denigration of others. Aunt Mildred was a poor, lonely, sick old lady who thought Jewel's home was ideal, loved Jewel's family, hated to have Jewel leave whenever she visited, and thought the world of Jewel.

The format of her tales usually included an ending in which she (and/or her family) emerged victorious and all others appeared corrupt and defeated.

But within her own positive self-description, there was room for sometimes soft, sometimes tough self-criticism. After she accidentally dropped one corner of the sheet, she exclaimed, "What's wrong with me?" Fumbling, "Can't even light a cigarette this morning."

Of herself, "Mean ole' mother. No wonder you want to go back to the hospital." She called herself "an impatient old woman."

"Well, today I get my (newspaper) and see how high my grocery bill will run this week. I guess David gets mighty sick of hearing all that crap." Jewel asked Chuck if he were about to study. He replied that he was. "I'll try to keep my mouth shut then." "Why don't you tell me to shut up?" Finally, she remarked one afternoon that Julie Ackerman looked "even uglier than I am."

Mrs. Smith's remarks indicated that she saw herself at times to be harsh, old, talkative, and ugly. There were indications, too, that she recognized her own periods of depression. For Jewel, too, suffered from depression. She handled it more skillfully than Chuck with denial, activity, and a sharp negativism that sought to externalize her problems, to keep the badness and sorrow "out there."

> Jewel was seated in the chair with her head in her hands, the picture of depression. Then her hands covered her face, her head still bowed. Chuck watched her silently. Finally, she shook herself into action, "Well . . . I've got to get this kitchen straightened up."
>
> She sat with her forehead in her hand. Chuck asked, "What's the matter, Mama?" "Oh, I'm just relaxing a bit. Nothing wrong," she responded wearily. She straightened up and hummed a soft tune but continued to appear lost in her thoughts.
>
> Jewel said something to the effect that if it didn't stop being rainy and muggy "we're gonna rot." There were a few minutes of silence. She was sitting, staring down, looking depressed. She stirred and remarked how poorly planned these apartment buildings were. "It's really bad the way they throw these things together. The architects are trained. Why do they make such errors?" Chuck replied, "It's easier to see things wrong when you're an observer than when you're doing something. You get involved . . ."

Other signs of Jewel's depression included fatigue ("I'm tired again. I just wouldn't be able to hold a regular job and I know it"), absolutism (She threw down the screwdriver. "Nothing's going right!"), and the self-criticism noted above.

The two sorts of indirect self-destructive behavior observed in Jewel seemed less aimed at self-harm than at her pervasive resistance to outside control. She forgot sometimes to take her heart medication *as scheduled by her physician*, and she pulled out an electric plug with wet hands, not wishing to take time to dry them.

Jewel's habit of shifting from a bright topic to a gloomy one deserves particular mention. As has been shown, this pattern parallels an important symptom element in Chuck's schizophrenia.

> "You can get the truth from the *Examiner*. But the *Times*, they distort everything according to politics."
>
> Jewel told a story of kindness—a plant gift from a lady she had never seen. Then she wished she didn't like plants so much because she had no place to put them.
>
> Chuck said, "There are so many (singing) groups out now." Jewel responded, "And they can't sing."
>
> "Rome is beautiful, but the Romans are the most cold, callous . . . people I've ever seen!"
>
> In the store, Jewel commented on the beautiful plants for sale, then she said that one of her ferns had died.
>
> Jewel told me of the enjoyment involved when the family got together to make ice cream. But the ice cream machine was broken and unfixable now.
>
> "He's one of the few Italians I like—a nice fellow, not like most young people these days. He's clean. His roommate was a filthy pig."

The shadowing researcher began to wince in anticipation of the coming critical barb whenever Jewel praised or spoke favorably about something. Of course, she had spoken favorably about DKR in his presence. What unspoken criticisms were in the back of her mind?

JEWEL'S OTHER TACTICS

Each person develops his own style of getting others to do what he wishes them to do. From requests and orders, to hints and provision of information that might influence others' choices of activity, humans have devised a plethora of tactics for gentle and heavy-handed manipulations. We have examined some of Jewel's direct efforts at control of others. Some of her more subtle tactics were aimed at control of mentally disturbed people.

Conscious Praise

On the morning of February 28th, Jewel praised Chuck while comparing his character with his brother's "stubborn and cantankerous" qualities. The message was clear: do not be hard for me to handle, Chuck. A few days later, both parents heaped praise on Chuck for catching four fish. It seemed as if they were augmenting their response in order to boost his self-image and to encourage Chuck to engage in any constructive pursuit. But the praise was sometimes directed toward the Chuck of the past, with the implied unfavorable evaluation of the Chuck of the present. "I was so proud of him." Again and again she spoke of how good he *used to* look, how talented and popular he *was*, the rescues he *made* as a lifeguard, his strength *in the past*.

Dishonesty

Jewel considered it expedient to lie to persons who were mentally disordered. That she made public her use of this tactic undermined some of her credibility in dealings with Chuck. Clearly, if she felt it was for his good, she would have no hesitation about telling an untruth. She reported responding to the query of an ex-prize fighter who "wasn't all there" that his terrible, slovenly clothes looked quite good. She admitted to lying but "in his condition, that was fine." When her sister was depressed, she asked Jewel if she had ever considered suicide. Jewel told her she had "so she wouldn't feel all by herself; but it was a lie."

Keeping Busy

With her depressed sister, as with Chuck, Mrs. Smith endeavored to keep them occupied. "We are going all out of our way to give her something to do—to get her mind off of herself." Similarly, her goal with Chuck was "Keep him busy. When he's preoccupied [sic] he doesn't have time to think." She considered her efforts to engage Chuck in "fix-it" jobs "a lot of bother but it sure beats him sitting around."

Indirection

It is often difficult to ascertain the interwoven threads of intent supporting a statement. There were occasions, however, when Jewel seemed to be instructing or admonishing Chuck in a roundabout way. For example, in the midst of a general discussion on the faults of our nation, she exclaimed, "God knows, I'd hate to be on welfare!" Again, in a conversation about an old friend, "There's a lot of people who think the world owes them a living." Chuck listened silently in both instances without response. On the day she wanted us out of the apartment so she could clean, she extolled the virtues of Donna's apartment for studying and emphasized the importance of Chuck's studies. Sometimes her implications were only lightly veiled, as in her comment about the typical mental patient. "When he comes out of the hospital, he isn't ready to work. (His parents) know that, and he does, too. It must be depressing to ask his parents for money for gas, school books, and things like that. He's draining the heck out of his parents and some of them just can't afford it."

Jewel herself recognized this tactic. She considered it preferable to drop hints rather than to nag. It might be argued that Jewel herself was as much controlled as she was controlling, that Jewel was adapting to *her* environment, which consisted of a household with a sarcastic, resistant husband and a mentally ill, suicidal son and that her existence was humdrum and unexciting. Chuck may have "controlled" her with his suicidality, his tentative emotional state, his low breaking point, and his own responses devised to subvert her domination. There are, for each of us, restrictions, demands, expectations, and requirements within which we live. The interactions between Mrs. Smith and Chuck were now complementary, and Chuck was able to "dominate" his mother to a minimal degree with the coping mechanisms he had developed. The pattern was clear, however. Mrs. Smith was not dominating *because* Chuck was resistant. To dominate and to control was her interpersonal style; people around her adapted to her. She may have adjusted some of her behavior to the responses she evoked, but she did not change her style.

MR. SMITH: BARBS AND BANTER

Charles, Sr., Chuck's father, threw up a battery of defenses against Jewel's control. His style utilized humor and aggressive thrusts, followed by quick retreats, covered by dry, artificial submission. He was the only family member who could coax into operation the family radio with its loose tubes and short circuits. From his perspective, "Radios are like wives—you've got to humor 'em."

The following represents a typical exchange between Chuck's parents. One evening Jewel was angry with the neighbors next door because they tapped on the wall, indicating that we were too noisy.

Jewel's righteous indignation started to inflate with her words. Charles, Sr., began agreeing with her, exaggerating his agreement and the correctness of her countercharges against the neighbors to the point of absurdity. She turned her irritation toward him. "Don't get 'horsey' with *me*," he deflated her. Soon she was engaged in a playful swatting fight with Chuck, a lesser opponent.

Both parents enjoyed their aggressive, joking exchanges, starting right out with them on several mornings. Mr. Smith's dry wit kept his wife entertained, kept her complaints focused on specific issues, and offered her a lighter perspective on her problems. She sometimes called him a "little boy" and told him to stop, but her next critical and controlling remark would prompt him to "start up" again. Sometimes his father's outlook would spill over to Chuck, and he would engage his mother in a mannered version of these lively debates. Chuck remembered these family joking exchanges as relatively recent substitutes for destructive family arguments.

Sometimes Charles, Sr., would enter the fray in order to take some of the heat off Chuck. One evening Jewel was left with the job of putting the table away after dinner. She berated Chuck for failing to help her. Chuck did not respond. Knowing full well that she had finished the chore, Mr. Smith (with mock husbandship) volunteered to help her with it. She turned on him, laughing.

Mr. Smith handled Jewel's self-praise in much the same way that he handled her attempted domination. He was constantly engaged in complimenting her, but in such an exaggerated, dry manner that it was apparent the compliments were insincere. If she reacted to the tone, he replied, hurt, that he could not understand what he had *said* that might upset her. He would play a role of humble innocence with elaborate unbelievability, engulfing her critical barbs with plush blandness. Sometimes the hostility underlying these exchanges would briefly surface through the glaze of humor, and both parents would verbally arch their backs and snap in overt competition. Then Mr. Smith would sugarcoat his words with wry humor and the angry contest would disguise itself again.

Only when Chuck's father was ill did he submerge "his usual mischief and wisecracks," as Jewel described them. She assessed this reduction in his dry sarcasm as a diagnostic indicator of his health and energy level, as a sort of primitive assessment of libido. One morning Chuck made a quipping comeback. Jewel perceived, "You sure are feeling better, for a change." Clearly, she used the same evaluative scale for both husband and son. When the smiling resistance was not forthcoming, it was obvious that Jewel missed it. She enjoyed the contests, finding no pleasure leaning up against thin air.

Charles, Sr., was still a rather good-looking man. One could imagine the strikingly handsome couple the Smiths must have been in the early years of their marriage. Chuck and Jewel were asked independently why Mr. Smith carried his arm at a strange angle. Each responded that they did not notice it anymore, and they offered two different stories about how it had been broken. Chuck thought that a truck accident had been the cause, but Jewel knew that the disfigurement occurred as the result of a fall from the porch during her husband's childhood. Although Mr. Smith had considered having it rebroken and reset, his wife had vetoed the idea, fearing complications.

From Jewel's point of view, her husband had always been too generous, too "freehearted," and too freespending. In the grocery store, for example, whatever the price, "he says, 'Go ahead and get it.' He just plays into their hands." Chuck recalled earlier days of anger, violence, and alcoholism in both parents. He had seen them mellow with age and with their abstinence from alcohol. Perhaps it was the aging itself or their approaching new opponent, death, that caused them to reevaluate their lives and ease up a bit.

The following vignette characterizes Charles, Sr.'s, interaction with the most important person in his life, Jewel. He hinted that he would like some tea. Jewel jumped up to prepare it, exaggerating her prompt response to the suggestion, caricaturing the submissive wife role. As she stood in the kitchen, she remarked in passing that the television volume was too high, causing her husband to get up to lower it. While he was up, he changed the channel to a program of his choice. And so it went.

CHUCK SMITH: RESISTANCE AND REBELLION

Each family member had developed characteristic ways of circumventing Jewel's domination. The efforts at asserting autonomy were not consistent, of course. In any interaction with another person, we engage in an intricately patterned dance, now bowing to his desires and pressures, now stepping out in concert with his movements, now leaping forward with our own intent pulling him along—resisting, mimicking, submitting, leading—the dance of shifting control. But, of course, in nearly every situation Jewel preferred to lead.

Chuck had developed various and ingenious tactics of response to Jewel's incessant pressure. Perhaps his simplest tactic was avoidance. By reading, sleeping and feigning sleep, by spending long periods at Donna's apartment, and by retiring to bedroom or bathroom, Chuck was able to withdraw spatially and psychologically from situations in which Jewel had the opportunity to exert control. It was no coincidence that, when Jewel would leave the apartment, Chuck's book would be put away or he would awaken. The avoidance tactic showed clearly one afternoon as Mrs. Smith ladled steaming criticisms about stores, impolite managers, filthy merchandise, and sale items nowhere to be found on the shelves. Chuck rose from the couch and went into the bathroom.

Chuck's second line of defense was to ignore Jewel's demands. Ignoring gave way to delayed response in many situations. For example, when Jewel wanted Chuck to get up so she could clean the bedroom, he would stay in bed longer than usual. On two different occasions, when she noted his need to wash, Chuck waited an hour before showering. Three minutes after a direct request to help in the kitchen, Chuck responded. Chuck was able at least to exert some influence over the timing of accession to his mother's demands.

Chuck had other tactics for circumventing Jewel's domination. On one occasion, she called Chuck at Donna's apartment to inform him that a favorite television program would be on at a certain time. The implication was that she expected Chuck to come home to watch it. Chuck accepted the information, made no commitment as to what he would do with it, and stayed at Donna's apartment. At another time, Chuck called Jewel from Donna's apartment telling her he would be home early (effectively short-circuiting her opportunity to ask him to do so). Then he promptly went to sleep and eventually got home late. Another tactic, to be discussed later in detail, involved Chuck's keeping important areas of his life secret from his mother to circumvent her control over them. Chuck's previous suicide attempts, medication and other drug usage, and his topless-bar hangout are examples of these hidden "free" areas.

Direct challenge of Mrs. Smith's controlling efforts was more characteristic of Mr. Smith's style than of Chuck's, but direct challenges were not totally absent from Chuck's repertoire. "Anyway, you're probably pooped," Jewel said, implying that Chuck should rest. She, too, was planning to sleep soon. "Not really," Chuck replied, resisting.

Again, one evening Chuck moved to lie down on the floor in front of the television. Jewel told him not to sleep because she would serve dessert soon. He told her to wake him for dessert. "I will not," was her response. It was seemingly a standoff, but the interaction proceeded in a most enlightening way. Chuck dozed intermittently during the show, then when Mrs. Smith got up to prepare dessert, Chuck told her he did not want any. Thus, he removed from her control the decision to serve him or not. Jewel was provoked to an unusual response; she called him "sissy." Chuck wondered what she meant. Possibly Jewel perceived on some level that Chuck's not wanting dessert had disrupted the opportunity for a further clash of wills—a clash she fully intended to win. She needed to see Chuck as backing down and so called him "sissy."

On the whole, Chuck's direct resistance was most often of a token sort. For example, when his mother suggested that he walk to Boys' Market for some eggs, his response was that it was "too far." But he went.

THE FRUITS OF DOMINATION

In this unhappy situation, Mrs. Smith was genuinely concerned and confused. She wanted Chuck to get well. She responded hopefully and joyfully to any slight signs of his progress toward recovery. Her response, however, was seen by Chuck as another attempt to control him. Thus far his disturbance remained an area free from her domination. His hallucinations, his suicidality, even his medications were his to control. He worked to please her, but could not allow her the victory this appeasement would entail.

She wanted him to be strong, to be active, productive, successful. So he could not let himself be any of these.

OTHER FAMILY THEMES

Resistance and acquiescence were not the only available responses to attempted control. One could turn the manipulation into a game or contest. One could sidestep the challenge through secrets or deceit.

Or one could merge or identify with the manipulator until the controller and the controlled became one.

Games and Contests

Whenever she felt up to it, Jewel tried to engage Chuck in some sort of contest. She planned to "beat the pants off" him in a snowball fight. On another occasion, she and Chuck playfully threw crumpled cigarette packages at each other while she, smiling, pronounced him as mean as his daddy. Swatting him with rolled newspapers, sitting on him to make him move, tickling him, or bantering with him seemed to be initiated not so much for the opportunity to dominate and control but for the sake of the contest itself. Sometimes Chuck would ignore or otherwise avoid Jewel's challenges. She seemed disappointed then, as if an effort with special meaning had been rejected.

Perhaps Jewel was trying to strengthen her son by these contests. Perhaps she felt that he would strengthen his will and his resistance through these competitive exercises. After all, her husband kept his wit sharpened and his independence assured by playful struggling. The concept of "mental strength" was firmly anchored within the family belief system. The mind (much like a muscle) could be strong or weak. If weak, it was prone to the dangers of suicide, insanity, depression, ridicule, control by others, illness, and fatigue. Speaking of a man whose leg had been amputated, Jewel said, "He had a very strong mind or he'd have gone off the deep end." Again, she considered her drooping lack of energy the previous week to have been "mental," a response to her husband's flu. And Jewel was proud that, despite her years of smoking, X-rays showed no serious lung problems. "You see, my lungs are strong and can fight it."

Inner strength was a necessity in the Smith family. Each member had developed some bastions of character to hold his own against the aggressive pressures of the others, particularly against Jewel's attempts to control. It was understandable, then, that family members often evaluated psychological functioning along a dimension of strength versus weakness.

"(Jacques Cousteau) is so mentally strong."

"(Her grandchild) is so strong—mentally."

Jewel warned Donna not to push herself or she might have a

nervous breakdown. "My mind isn't that weak," was Donna's reply.

It cannot be denied that, during their playful contests, the Smith family showed a liveliness and creativity, a sharp independence and will to win that invigorated and refreshed even the tangential observer. But these moments of sparkling activity stood in bright contrast to the relentless struggle for power carried on unrecognized at a different level.

Secrets and Deceit

It can be argued that any group needs some minimal measure of secrets and deceit to function and survive. Certainly, no one has the time or desire to be wholly open and honest with others. At any moment our feelings and thoughts are so complex and conflicting that it is impossible to bare ourselves to others through the clumsy format of language. As for the secrets and deceits we impress upon ourselves, exposing those inner hidden recesses, even to ourselves, is at least a lifetime job. Here we attempt only to identify some of the simple omissions and fictions employed within the Smith family to various ends and purposes.

Chuck's three primary areas of secrecy were his frequenting of a nude bar, his occasional pot-smoking, and his maintaining a general level of inactivity. The first two areas were kept secret from his parents but not from his sister. His mother would "disown" him if she knew. The last area was not exposed to anyone, particularly not to hospital staff.

Chuck skillfully protected his contact with the nude bar. A television news special on nude bars drew only an occasional glance and a look of disinterest from him. Sometimes he invited Jewel to go shopping with him, believing she would refuse. If she responded as expected, he could go to the bar for an extended period under the pretext of "shopping." The cover story fell flat occasionally, as when Jewel smelled alcohol on Chuck's breath after his return from the "book store." The existence and nature of that particular bar, however, remained Chuck's secret.

Smoking marijuana was a rare occurrence compared with the twice-a-week visit to the bar, so it was relatively easily concealed. When his mother brought up the subject of pot-smoking, noting that the parents of the girls she thought were using it probably knew nothing about it, Chuck coolly responded that Donna had once smelled marijuana at a rock concert. Unaware of the sensitivity of the topic, Jewel moved on to another subject.

The extent to which Chuck slept, dozed, half-listened to records, and simply sat daydreaming was unknown to the significant others in his life, although some may have suspected. He moved cleverly from setting to setting, giving the impression in each that in the other settings he was busy and active. This tactic required that there be minimal understanding and interchange among the settings. Chuck's parents knew only vaguely what he did at Donna's apartment, at school, at the hospital, and, of course, knew nothing of what he did at the nude bar. Similarly, hospital staff members were presented with a false picture of moderate activity at home and school that they were eager to accept and were too busy to verify. As long as Chuck's life moved along smoothly, everyone seemed willing to allow Chuck to create their perception of his activities in these scattered settings.

We were not privy to other family members' secrets to the degree that we were to some of Chuck's. We knew of the parents' private discussions about Chuck's deteriorating condition, of Jewel's vaguely concealed concern about the signs she considered portents of another breakdown for Chuck, and of the parents' plan to surprise Chuck with a vacation financed by some of the money from the study.

Merging and Identification

When two people spend long periods of time together, it is not unusual to find one mirroring the characteristics of the other. Because we began observing the Chuck-Jewel dyad well along in the course of their relationship, we could not determine who had learned to imitate whom. There were, however, many interesting parallels that could be noted as we entered the scene.

There were moments when Chuck duplicated his mother's negativism. These words could have been spoken by Jewel, but they were Chuck's: "All you have to do is find something new, and pretty soon it'll be contaminated by people." Jewel's reinforcing response was ". . . it becomes dirt." Again, "It's getting to the point where almost everything you do is wrong these days." The latter quotation, uttered by Chuck, reflects Jewel's negativism and leans toward her characteristic absolutism as well. One day his mother was "tied up in knots" from tension; the next day Chuck complained of the same symptom. Mrs. Smith was observed several times sitting with head in hands, the living picture of Chuck's depression.

Chuck described one complex of symptoms to his psychiatrist as follows: everything was beautiful one moment and then everything became dark, like heaven and hell. He noted that this change occurred many times a day. Of course, we cannot demonstrate a direct connection between his perceptual/conceptual fluctuation and Jewel's similar oscillations in her speech. The parallel forms, however, are unquestionably intriguing. Her pattern of positive utterances immediately followed by negative, gloomy assertions has been described earlier.

THE DISORDER: SUICIDE AND SCHIZOPHRENIA

We have argued that Chuck Smith's symptoms were, in part, a response to his mother's attempts to dominate his life. They were *his* symptoms. Chuck's suicidality worried his mother. She would have liked to control that aspect of his life, too. But if Chuck were to give in and overcome his suicidal impulses, he would lose an important battle for control of his life. He preserved his autonomy in life by trying, now and again, to control his own death. Perhaps someday he would win that battle and lose his life.

There is very little in the literature beyond information about the *presence* or *absence* of symptoms in various diagnostic categories. Except for some autobiographic accounts, there is almost nothing specific about the patterning of symptoms over a day or a week, or about the situational responsiveness of their appearance. Whenever Chuck exhibited symptoms or reported their presence during the research period, they were recorded. In addition, a long-term perspective was provided by his parents and from hospital records.

In this section of the analysis, we first look at how Chuck described his inner experience, including his visual and auditory hallucinations, his feelings of depression, and his dreams. We then consider his parents' perspective on Chuck's problem behavior, and we briefly evaluate his extrafamilial relationships.

Visual Illusions

Visual hallucinations or illusions are relatively rare in schizophrenia. It was not clear to what degree Chuck's distortions of visual perception were due to his schizophrenia, his medication, or to a rather active, symbolizing imagination. Chuck remembered the distortions to have begun when he was eleven.

Anticipating difficulty on an algebra exam, Chuck escaped by going to his nude bar. There, a nude dancer turned into a large white egg with rat's legs. Two days later, as he awoke from his sleep, his father's face appeared distorted and blackened. At that time his depth perception was also somewhat affected. Exactly a week later, Chuck sat in class and saw his professor to be appropriately tall and wide but without depth, like a playing card. A girl seated about the same distance away also appeared flattened. Chuck admitted some control over the faces he saw coming out of walls. Further diminishing of the illusions was possible within an hour of taking Thorazine.

Drinking, too, probably had its effects on Chuck's visual perception of the world. Ordinary objects became "unreal." But Chuck's driving did not appear to be significantly impaired.

Although Chuck rejected the idea that alcohol altered his perception of reality, he did believe that Elavil made objects appear to be more distant and that medication distorted his visual perception in other ways. Again, Chuck demonstrated no little control over the effects of these distortions.

Auditory Hallucinations

Chuck's auditory hallucinations, though uniquely appropriate to his situation, were of a general type common to schizophrenics. They were primarily negative: "Don't change lanes!" "Don't read it!" "Hey!" "Knucklehead!" "Capitalist pig!"

It is easy to associate such voices with Jewel. She was heard telling him sharply not to change lanes; she did not want him to read magazines like *Playboy*; and one could readily imagine her shouting "Hey!" and "Knucklehead!"

The voices were at times calm and sexless despite their pejorative content. It was as if Chuck's mind had drained the emotion and identifying source from the content. Chuck could distinguish a feeling associated with the experience of hearing voices whether words were heard or not. He mentioned this feeling after revealing his nude bar visits to the researcher. The feeling was clearly associated with failure to live up to the perceived standards of someone else. The voice that said "cream rises to the top" could be understood in this context. Chuck was not rising anywhere. He was slipping into another relapse.

When one suffers from auditory and visual hallucinations, the credibility of one's own sensory output declines. Chuck poured hot water into a cup with what he thought was powdered instant coffee. The aroma of the mixture was more like bouillon. Chuck thought at first he was hallucinating, but he discovered that it actually was bouillon powder in the cup.

When an unexpected occurrence takes place, the locus of the incongruity may lie within us, or in the world about us, or in both. In this instance, Chuck's initial hypothesis was that the cause of the problem was his faulty sense perception system. This hypothesis exemplifies a common schizophrenic lack of confidence in the sensory "connections" to the real-world-out-there.

Depression

Depressions rarely involve a continuous lowered mood. For the patient reporting his symptoms to a therapist, it may seem that the preceding week or month has been an unending emotional swamp. When careful observation replaces colored recollection, however, we find much more fluctuation in mood than is usually conveyed by the static term "depressed state."

The month of our research included two periods of noticeable tension and depression for Chuck. His extreme nervousness was indicated by chain smoking, cracking knuckles, and a rocking of his body that he tried to control when he noticed it. Lying still on the couch to quiet himself produced little relief. He could not sleep, and his twitching toes sometimes revealed the presence of a furiously racing inner motor. His increased tension created a burning sensation in his stomach and brought a flushing heat to his skin. It is hard to ascertain how much of the latter was due to the increased doses of Thorazine he took to calm himself.

The first sign of his initial depression came ten days after his discharge. He felt "ambivalent" that morning, a forewarning of his turning mood. The depression bottomed out six nights later. On the next morning Chuck seemed to be in an elevated mood, but upon recounting his troubles to various staff people at the hospital that day he was significantly dejected again. By that evening, a waitress at the nude bar asked him what was the matter—he looked so depressed. The next morning Chuck told his parents of his two-pound weight loss.

About five days of a plateau state followed. Part of this may have been from a change in medication that distanced him temporarily from his environment and his feelings. Jewel began to feel nervous, perhaps in anticipation of Chuck's rapid slide back into the hospital. The young man could turn on some animation when interacting with friends, professionals, and shopkeepers outside of the home, but he often retreated into his defensive depression when he returned. Even within the apartment, he could indulge in an occasional quip, notice the beauty of the sky, and lose himself in reading.

All seemed to be going reasonably well, but on March 15th Chuck announced that he was "all tied up in knots." His complaints of nervousness continued during early morning. Gloom infiltrated his conversation. By the time he had begun packing to return to the hospital, he was in good spirits again. Certainly his signs and symptoms were less severe than those earlier in the month, but no hospitalization had resulted then. Chuck's money was running out. Perhaps the hospital with its activities and acquaintances began to attract him as an antidote to the poisonous boredom and inactivity of his lifelessness on the outside. Perhaps the forthcoming termination of the research project prompted his return to the hospital. His unexpectedly taking a candid photograph of DKR on the morning of readmission may have symbolized a wish that the relationship would continue past the ending of the project. At any rate, with his sheltered adventure on the outside completed, Chuck made it safely back to his institutional haven. For that purpose, his relapse was well timed and well used.

Dreams

During the month of our live-in research, Chuck reported a number of dreams. On the level of overt content and surface symbolism, the dreams dealt with important existential concerns: social-sexual relations, death, control, punishment, self-exposure, success, failure, and rescue. They pointed to key issues in Chuck's everyday lifestyle.

Three of the dreams had sexual themes. He dreamed of high school girls fenced in and kicking a tennis ball about. Later he was swinging. A fat girl walked in front of the swing. He caught her by spreading his legs and continued swinging with her. He dreamed one morning of a beautiful woman in the guise of a beggar. Following an evening at a nude bar, Chuck dreamed of nude women. On another occasion, Chuck dreamed that he became angry when his mother threw away his *Playboy* magazines. Clearly the area of sexuality and cross-sexual social contact was a frustrating one for Chuck. Although he claimed to have experienced normal contacts with females throughout high school and military service, his current encounters with accessible women were submerged in secrecy, deceit, artificiality, and vicarious fantasy. Chuck had no dates during the research period.

Two dreams seemed related to the study in progress. In one, someone kept taking photographs with a Polaroid camera but did not pull out the exposed prints for viewing. In a second dream, Chuck intended to play conservative music for some "vague" audience but played a sexier, wilder piece from *Hair*, the rock musical, instead. He did not notice the audience's reaction to this unintended exposure of another side of his musical taste. The latter dream occurred immediately after Chuck revealed his habit of going to a nude bar. Another dream was less clearly connected with the research, Chuck was told to drive into a river to rescue a baby (himself?) so that someone could photograph him in action.

Nearly every night Chuck dreamed of the military and the theater, both representing important episodes in his life. The former was a time of independence from his family but of tight control by others. The latter was a time of success and hope for Chuck but may also have symbolized impermanence and artificiality. Related to the military was Chuck's dream of becoming a four-star general just before his fifth admission to the psychiatric hospital.

A final pair of dreams is worth noting. From a distance created by flying and LSD, Chuck could look down on the earth and see that it (his life) was hell. In the second dream, a curfew man (his father?) caught Chuck out after curfew and machine-gunned him. Certainly, failure to live up to family norms provoked instant verbal abuse when it was detected.

His Parents' Perspective

Part of the frustration for Jewel and Charles, Sr., came from their recognition of Chuck's unfulfilled potential, from their contrast of Chuck in the present with Chuck in the past. They could tell story after story of Chuck's past successes, but each story only underscored the difference between then and now. When Jewel expressed the wish that Chuck could be his old self all the time, she implied that he could not. He *used to* look so good; he *used to* do things that made her proud. Her husband's frustration would simmer over occasionally. He would remark that Chuck was "lazy," that he would be "like he is" until he got up "off his butt." Mrs. Smith sometimes blamed the difference between Chuck's past and present on his drinking. Chuck was "another person" when drinking, said Jewel. Alcohol is a depressant, she had learned, and it depressed him. Furthermore, she worried about what might happen to him and to an innocent victim when Chuck drove under the influence of alcohol.

Both parents felt the burden of responsibility for providing Chuck with various kinds of support. Chuck appeared to respond not only with ingratitude, taking for granted their sincere efforts, but with occasional accusations that they were too much in the foreground, too controlling in his life. He drew on their limited resources of living space, time, physical effort, and money. In the past, they had driven him places even though it was a strain on them. Jewel knew Chuck sensed the strain ("Am I right, Chuck?" He agreed.). They moved him from apartment to apartment. He was "underfoot" when Jewel wanted to clean. Furthermore, Jewel believed Chuck's problems contributed to her heart trouble. He also embarrassed her by lying all day on the couch with the curtains open, presenting an unacceptable image to the neighbors.

The message got across to Chuck through various channels that he was an encumbrance, that he was in the way:

> She said she could get a lot of housework done. "I'll be here by myself and not have anybody in the way." Chuck said, "You mean I'm in the way—well, thanks a lot."
> "This place won't do (i.e., it's too small). If you'll behave yourself and stay home (i.e., stay out of the hospital) we can move." Chuck replied, "I'd wait a while before I moved." Jewel agreed, "We depended on you too many times before. We'll wait."

Later, his mother kidded Chuck that sometimes she did not know if he were worth the trouble he had been. Surely the messages were destructive. But the reasons for his parents' anger and frustration must not be overlooked. The Smiths as a resource had been drained over and over with no noticeable positive response from Chuck. They argued that they could not build their lives around their son, but in many ways they did.

They hoped throughout that Chuck would maintain interest and money enough to stumble along to a college degree. They hoped also that someone would discover a curative medicine one day that would allow Chuck to regain and to develop the potential he had once exhibited.

In the meantime, what could they do that would be therapeutic for their son? They were in a bind because suggestions or advice were interpreted as attempts to infantilize him or to run his life. Jewel tried to make Chuck feel useful. When aware of what she was doing, she tried to avoid probing into his activities even if she knew something were wrong. She tried to cheer him with jokes and hopeful newspaper horoscopes, but her efforts were so obviously effortful that they often backfired. Of course, Chuck could have taken them in the spirit of helpful sustenance in which they were offered, but the ensconced pattern of domination continued to characterize the Smith household, touching each action and each statement with its wand of power, snuffing out the glow of gentle concern.

EXTRAFAMILIAL RELATIONS

The hours Chuck Smith spent in contact with any persons outside of his family were insignificant compared with the hours he spent interacting with family members, particularly with his mother. The hospital offered a pool of peer acquaintances and a few concerned professionals, and there were some other settings in which Chuck socialized routinely.

Hospital Links

The psychiatric hospital had become Chuck's second home. On the day of his discharge, staff members and patients gave him their personal best wishes for success on the outside. Chuck considered the event much like graduation from high school, but his relations with these people were not severed by discharge. Dr. Harrison, a psychologist, continued to see him in scheduled group-therapy sessions and afterward as they walked together to her car. She was the person to whom Chuck turned with his deepest personal concerns. She was his wise and understanding therapist, a professional friend in the finest sense.

Ms. Barbara Bristol was a social worker who also influenced Chuck's life. Ms. Bristol was more confronting, more "hardnosed" in a uniquely humorous way. She could probe, doubt, even criticize with a style that kept her helping quality up front. She was another good woman in Chuck's life. It was Ms. Bristol who remarked to Chuck that he seemed to enjoy his depression. She, of all his professional acquaintances, was most aware of the secondary gratifications of Chuck's disturbance. She was eager to have Chuck try a living situation away from his family, sensing his difficulty in establishing a new life pattern within the setting that sustained a familiar one. Barbara Bristol invited Chuck back to the hospital and arranged his readmission when Chuck was in need of such assistance.

Chuck's relationships with others in the hospital seemed less supportive. Several of the patients were acquaintances, ready to sit and talk—what else was there to do? With Chuck present or absent, however, their lives were not significantly altered. The staff on Chuck's home ward recognized him, but they were busy and not inclined to carry on a conversation. In the ward meeting for outpatients, staff seemed concerned with keeping patients in their place, eliciting artificial but "proper" speeches from patients and avoiding genuine issues and conflicts. Chuck attended that group because attendance was expected of him and because people would worry if he were absent. His reasons for being there coincided with the empty tone of the group itself.

Chuck's interaction with medical staff was characterized by unreasoning effort on both sides. The medical system required all sorts of circumlocutions to prove itself even marginally workable. Chuck's physician based his decisions on inaccurate information from the start. For example, Chuck spoke of "hallucinations," but the word had special meaning in Chuck's instance. He commonly used the word to mean "visual illusions," but during interviews both patient and doctor used the word without knowing how the other intended it. Furthermore, hospital records were in error. For example, in his case file, a nurse described Chuck's Moog music (which she misunderstood to be "mood" music) as depressing. Although it was weird, electronically-created music, it was certainly lively and happy in mood. So, based on misinformation about Chuck's lifestyle, his symptoms, and his medications (some of which Chuck did not take), the psychiatrist made *medical* responses to Chuck's difficulties by endlessly adjusting and readjusting medications and dosages to deal with Chuck's "illness." Then he gave unclear instructions that Chuck could not repeat ten minutes after hearing them.

For Chuck to reenter the ward of his choice, he had to present himself as reasonably disturbed (so as to assure rehospitalization) but not disturbed enough to wind up in a locked ward. The system was a foe, comprising a set of boundaries and rules that required delicate maneuvering and manipulation to achieve a desired, therapeutic outcome.

Other Outsiders

Chuck's interactions with shopkeepers, mechanics, and salespeople were perhaps slightly warmer than the superficial coolness common to our cultural handling of these contacts. Chuck disliked the robot-like, stereotypical exchanges he sometimes encountered, such as when he asked a salesperson if he thought it would rain that night. "No, we close at 10:00 P.M. on Saturday and Sunday," was the unhearing reply.

Relationships with the waitress-dancers in the nude bar were casual, almost impersonal, although some did know his name and one waitress expressed concern when he looked depressed. There was no denying the economic basis to the interactions, however. The dancing provided escape and glittering fantasy material and, as Chuck put it, "This sure beats looking at those hospital walls."

DISCUSSION: PROCEDURES AND PROCESS

As has been described, the tactic of shadowing involves living alongside someone during nearly all of his waking hours, observing and recording his verbalized thoughts and his activities. Such a research procedure generates unique complications, and important questions and issues were raised by our research with the Smith family. How did family members perceive the research? Did the participants feel it necessary to "play to" the anthropologist as to an audience? What specific techniques were useful in keeping DKR disengaged from family interactions? What difficulties and failures were encountered as DKR tried to maintain a posture of nonparticipation? How did the research affect DKR, and how could these effects be used to generate hypotheses and understandings?

Family Perception of the Research

From the beginning, Chuck made no attempt to conceal the investigator's presence or purpose. "He's studying me," was a typical response to a query about DKR's identity. The study gave Chuck some prestige in hospital circles. When asked at the outset how he liked participation in such a project, Chuck replied, "It's kind of fun." To be sure, the pleasurable aspects of participation varied from moment to moment, but the family seemed to enjoy the companionship that the researcher provided even though the participatory function of a genuine companion was sometimes lacking. In the early phase, DKR was concerned with the issue of privacy to the degree that he sometimes offered to leave when Chuck was engaged, for example, in a personal phone call. But Chuck consistently responded to such offers by inviting him to stay, so eventually it was agreed that if Chuck felt that he needed some "space" he should take the initiative and tell DKR freely. Perhaps knowing that he had such an option made exercising it unnecessary. On one occasion, however, knowing that DKR was about to shower, Chuck left the apartment for about ninety minutes. On that day he appeared troubled, and both Jewel and DKR interpreted his timing of the exit as indicating that he wanted to separate himself from the research for a short while. Considering that Chuck was under observation for almost all of his waking hours for an entire month (reporting on those hours that were not directly observed), he showed high tolerance for this sort of intrusion into his life.

From the outset, it was agreed that any family member could read the ongoing field notes. Reynolds kept as many as three or four days' logs with him until he could drop them off at his office or apartment for safekeeping. About a week after his discharge, Chuck and Donna read the notes. Donna continued to show interest in what was written for another week or so, but her interest dwindled, too, as she encountered a repetitive record of similar family events, not edited for smoothness and style. The parents did not read the journal, perhaps because they did not want to appear overly inquisitive. Knowing that their children had read the material and had no objections to it, they were probably satisfied that it was reasonably accurate and inoffensive.

Relating to a Family Researcher

Acceptance of an outsider in their midst took time and it varied somewhat among the family members. Guest status passed in less than a week, but the amorphous role of observer was problematic for family members. For example, throughout the research Jewel continued to refer to Charles, Sr., as "my husband" to DKR but as "Dad" or "Daddy" to other family members. Nonetheless, signs of growing attachment were manifest. Jewel hoped that DKR would maintain contact with the family after the research was completed. Furthermore, when Chuck was about to return to the hospital, Jewel hugged DKR and told him to tell Chuck that she loved him. Chuck's father maintained man-to-man distance, shaking hands at the final exit and making "proper" responses throughout. Donna interacted with DKR much as she would with any of her brother's friends. Of all the family members, Chuck took most advantage of this opportunity to reveal himself and to establish a unique relationship. His acceptance of DKR almost reached the point of identification. He mimicked his gestures and habits, as will be detailed later, and he signed a note to his mother "Love, Chuck and David." He felt comfortable enough to put a butter knife playfully to DKR's neck and to punch him in the stomach, and he joked that his quiet shadow was "always depressed."

On the night before his readmission, Chuck asked DKR to stay at the family apartment. On the last day, he took a candid photo of DKR, a permanent image to remind of the shadowing researcher's presence. The journal holds numerous instances of self-revelation indicating the trust and satisfaction Chuck found in the relationship with DKR. His dreams revealed some perplexity about the processing and interpreting of what he was sharing, but mutual acceptance was maintained.

Techniques of Disengagement

Specific tactics were used to participate as unobtrusively as possible in Chuck's life. The objective of these tactics was to accustom the family to the constant presence of the recording researcher. Reynolds sat in a chair distanced from their interaction whenever possible. Almost always, a book or writing materials were in his hands. Family members probably could not determine whether he was reading or listening, writing letters or taking notes, tape recording or not, attending to their ongoing interaction or not, nor did they care particularly within a very short while. Of course, when DKR was pulled into a conversation it was apparent that he was attending to the family at that moment.

In his attempts to remain inconspicuous, he did not adopt the role of the absolutely silent observer. To do so would have made the researcher uncomfortable, and probably the family as well. When attempts were made to get DKR to reveal what was happening in Chuck's life, he would evade the query by directing it to Chuck. Of course, when Reynolds knew Chuck was lying or misleading others, he did not volunteer that information to anyone.

When Chuck sought his opinion on a subject, DKR almost always was able to sidestep the issue. In addition, he made it clear that the sidestepping was done intentionally and purposefully. Usually Reynolds did not eat or mention eating when Chuck skipped a meal. When Chuck waited in a long line although a shorter one was nearby, or when he waited in a wrong line, or when he spent his meager income on unnecessarily high-priced items, DKR did not comment. Reynolds learned to follow Chuck through doors, to stand when he stood, and to sit when he sat so as not to control the timing of Chuck's interactions with others. The shadowing observer was able to slip away only when Chuck was asleep and return before he awakened. On these few occasions, DKR was able to sleep in his own apartment after waiting for Chuck to go to bed and then return early the next morning.

When Chuck suggested doing anything together, DKR agreed. Reynold's preferences were stated broadly, if at all, and only after others had made their preferences known. To be sure, this posture was imperfect. But Jewel spontaneously commented near the end of the study, "David just won't commit himself. . . . He just won't become involved." Chuck also remarked later that Reynolds was extremely passive and nondirective.

The Difficulties of Nonparticipation

There were cracks and holes in the blank wall that DKR attempted to present to the Smith family. Every researcher must strike a compromise position based on ideal research conditions on the one hand and the needs of his subject and himself on the other. The first area in which the researcher became an active directing participant was the area of safety and health. On two occasions, following some moderate drinking by Chuck, DKR drove them home. Again, when DKR noticed that Chuck was about to back into another car, he gave warning. Finally, on a cold night when Chuck slept uncovered on Donna's living room floor, DKR put two blankets over him. The conditions requiring intervention did not extend to times when Chuck was hallucinating while driving or when he failed to eat or to take his medication. In those situations, DKR simply recorded the phenomena and remained silent.

Another area of active participation was prompted by situations requiring reciprocity. Although the family was paid for DKR's room and board, he still felt some desire to repay them further when appropriate. At the movie, for example, Donna bought popcorn for the three attending. Chuck bought a round of soft drinks, and so did DKR. He also helped Donna with her income tax forms. When asked, he brought to Chuck a subscription form from one of his issues of *Psychology Today*.

Although an attempt was made to limit the shadow's direct influence on the family system, there was no question that the information fed back into the system by the anthropologist altered it in important ways. For example, Chuck inquired about the stresses that had been observed up to one point in the study and received a wide-ranging, honest reply. He read the observation notes on a couple of occasions. He listened as DKR talked with Donna and Jewel about the research. Rarely, general advice was offered when elicited by a family member. Several times an interpretation of an event that differed from Chuck's came to light. At least once, DKR verbalized his disagreement with Jewel's interpretation of the basis for Chuck's insecurity. And twice, near the end of the study period, DKR made explicit attempts to direct Chuck's thinking about the subject of suicide and to reinforce recognition of Chuck's abilities through praise. The perceptive reader will find many other examples of direct and indirect effects throughout the journal, in spite of Reynolds's efforts to minimize them.

These interventions spotlighted the conflict between study goals and treatment goals. Some interventions were prompted by concerns for health and safety; other decisions to intervene were based on evaluations of informational and behavioral needs. If it appears that Reynolds was profligate in his wielding of influence in this area, let it be said that for every impulse that resulted in input, ten impulses were quelled. Models of influence were rife in Chuck's life settings.

But intervention resulted not only from such noble conflicts. There were times when the researcher was tired, when he forgot his passive role, when his own physical comfort dictated opening the door to a stuffy apartment or asking Chuck if he felt chilly. The researcher led a dual life, with one side devoted to the research and another side scaled down considerably but still requiring attention to mail, to paying bills, and to socializing. His own values and needs influenced him to stop accompanying Chuck to the nude bar after several joint visits demonstrated to him the stereotypical quality of Chuck's interactions there.

In one notable way DKR, however careful, could not help but affect Chuck. He provided a model of an alternate lifestyle. Some areas that seemed to attract imitative behavior in Chuck included notebook writing, drink preference, use of a noncommittal verbal response ("Hmmmm"), and certain lying and sitting positions. Of course, there were many other areas and models available to Chuck. From reports of family members and from hospital records, it appears that Chuck's general life-style remained essentially unchanged in spite of the shadowing researcher and the other disturbances to his interaction systems.

Some of these interactions probably changed the course of life events for Chuck in substantial ways. Most of them probably did not. We have included specific details so that the reader can assess the anthropologist's impact on Chuck's life during this interim period between hospitalizations. On the whole, it would appear that the shadowing observer had relatively little effect on Chuck's life, although the effect could not be called nonexistent. What about the effect of the Smith family on the observer?

Effect on Shadowing Observer

Reynolds had never encountered such internal resistance to rereading (the journal material) and writing (about the Smith family). Sighs and avoidance behavior underlined his unreadiness to reexperience those depressing days of conscious self-control. During the research, he had felt mentally and physically sluggish as a result of his sedentary life while living alongside Chuck. In time, he could doze off at will during the day. Hours passed rather quickly this way. A sort of personal numbness along with an unreal quality to the world helped to cushion the steady undermining of optimism and hope experienced in the Smith household.

Sometimes DKR would struggle against the pervasive boredom and meaninglessness of Chuck's way of life. He had the sense that they were only waiting, but waiting with no major goal in mind except, perhaps, death. He would sometimes surreptitiously carry out isometric exercises, and he thoroughly enjoyed the short walks entailed by some errands. His own values would intrude again and again to spark sadness or anger in response to Chuck's easy, nonproductive life. He could empathize in some moments with Chuck's father, who wanted Chuck to "get off his butt."

On two occasions DKR felt fear. Once, upon reflection, after Chuck had put his arm around DKR's neck and a butter knife to his throat, and once when DKR and Chuck were sleeping in the same apartment with no one else around. The fears may have been unfounded, but they illuminated the limits of the researcher's trust in this man who had made serious attempts on his own life.

Twice DKR felt worry that Chuck might do himself harm combined with guilt that he was not with him at potentially dangerous points in his life. In both instances, DKR hurried back to check on Chuck's well-being.

There were moments of conflict, particularly when Mrs. Smith tried to pump DKR for information about Chuck's activities outside the apartment. Jewel was an important person in the family, perhaps the most influential member. The observer could afford neither to antagonize her nor to compromise Chuck's trust in his ability to protect the confidentiality of certain events. Directing her queries to Chuck relieved some of the pressure.

The researcher learned a great deal about himself and his own needs and tendencies by deliberately frustrating them. He wanted to share his thoughts with others but could not. His scheduled eating and sleeping patterns were disrupted. He caught himself subtly cuing others to his desires in various ways before eliminating such signaling behaviors in the research context. For example, when he asked

Chuck if he felt cold, DKR realized that he expected Chuck to ask him the same question. DKR could then respond that he was cold and could thereby effect change through his query. Shifts in his sitting position sometimes signaled boredom or indicated what he perceived to be the end of an interaction. These shifts had to be monitored.

Certain of DKR's own responses were revealing and were important to the findings of the study. By living alongside Chuck and by imitating his behaviors, DKR was able to gain some of what the Japanese call "taiken" (body-knowledge) of Chuck Smith's world. For example, when Jewel began a positive or neutral sentence, DKR caught himself wincing. This made him aware of her pattern of positive beginnings and pessimistic dark endings to utterances. Jewel's rapid switching from soft, loving tones to sharp, harsh tones with her grandchildren startled and upset DKR, suggesting hypotheses for their effects on the grandchildren and probably on Chuck's childhood, as well. He found himself carefully censoring his own behavior to avoid the immediate criticism to which every family member was subject. Politeness became a bubble of protection with which he surrounded himself, just as the family members seemed to do.

His expectations about future events and family reactions were often confirmed, thus building confidence in his understanding of family relationships and habits. Even his dreams during the research period spoke of mood swings and hallucinatory voices, impressions of his unconscious estimation of craziness. Margaret Mead has stated that the researcher is his own most sensitive and effective instrument. Shadowing magnifies this potential.

Implications

Participation as close observer in a month of another person's life is an uncommon privilege. We have no equivalent nonfiction descriptions of "normal" lifestyles and family interactions and little likelihood of soon obtaining such descriptions. Only people who are hurting, people who hope for improvement in their lot or for protection from themselves, are willing to risk exposure of their everyday existence to the shadowing researcher.

This sort of study cannot be replicated precisely. One cannot have both the nonintrusive observation of the Smith family in their natural setting and the situational control necessary for experimental replication. Nevertheless, the repeated clinical observations of psychologists and the anthropological participant-observation records of patterned behaviors are the results of naturalistic replication. In naturalistic replication, the controls are exerted by the setting and the participants rather than by the researcher. In a broader sense, of course, even experimental design can be seen to present a special case of naturalistic replication, with the experimenter as one of the participants, constrained as any subject is constrained by rules and habits both inside and outside of his awareness.

Among the naturalistic observations of shadowing, prediction of outcomes is possible. We have called these predictions minihypotheses. For example, when Chuck determined to lose weight, we predicted that Jewel would try to take control of Chuck's effort by putting him on a diet or by sabotaging his purpose with fattening foods. The next morning Jewel invited Chuck to go on a diet with her and her husband after the research was over. She attempted to control not only the diet but its timing. Similarly, predictions that Jewel's utterances would begin neutrally or positively and would end negatively were generally fulfilled. Such confirmations of minihypotheses give the observers confidence in their understanding of events and participants.

THE USES OF SCHIZOPHRENIA

Some of the ways in which schizophrenia becomes a useful pattern of emotional disturbance can be understood on the basis of our study of the Smith family. Although we write here of schizophrenia, many other patterns, such as suicidality and various kinds of somatic and psychological disorders, can be put to similar use. We are not dealing with the issue of what we believe schizophrenia to *be* but rather with how it can be (and was) *used*.

Schizophrenia offers protection. In the critical, challenging atmosphere of the Smith family, subjective statements labeled as such were safe: "it seems so to me . . ."; "I feel . . ."; "It looked (to me) as if . . ." could not be challenged in any obvious way. Schizophrenia involves a personal, subjective perspective to an extreme degree. Who could challenge the validity of what the schizophrenic says the hallucinatory voices told him? Who could argue with Chuck about his stated experience of tension and depression? Sometimes Chuck purposely used this uncontestable subjectivity to "put on" his mother, to fool her. He also used it to ensure his return to the hospital (and to a desirable ward in the hospital).

Schizophrenia also provided Chuck with some protective distance from Jewel's smothering control. Outside his parents' household was a dangerous world with harsh rules and quick punishment. It was populated by uncaring robots, each concerned with protecting himself. Within the family was safety, leisure, and concern, but also stifling pressure. The problem Chuck faced was to maintain both shelter and distance. This he did with great skill.

Another hypothesis that emerged from our observations concerned the contribution to psychological functioning of physical movement or lack of it. The interrelationship is likely to be circular rather than unidirectional, but it appears that moderate activity and movement from place to place may enhance one's perception of multiple solutions to problems, in a manner analogous to the shifting perspective provided by changes in spatial position. At one extreme, inactivity may promote a narrowed perspective on problems, resulting in the perception of single or very few solutions. At the other extreme, constant movement may promote perception of so many alternatives that indecision in the area of personal problems may result. These three activity-cum-perception models correspond to normalcy, depression, and agitated depression, respectively. It may be that therapeutic manipulation of physical activity can contribute to an improved functional perspective on life problems.

AFTERWORD

On April 5th, after the live-in phase of the research was completed, the investigators met with members of the Smith family (Charles, Sr., Jewel, and Chuck) to discuss the study.

Jewel began by saying, "We thoroughly enjoyed David; we accepted him as part of the family."

Mr. Smith offered his opinion that "It would've been better if there had been more room for David to sleep. Except for when my wife and I are here alone, it's crowded."

Jewel picked up on her husband's comment. "There's no void for Chuck to fill in our cubbyhole." She seemed to equate physical space with void. "In some families the mother is away, the father is working, and maybe there are no brothers and sisters nearby. They may be better off financially, but in such families there is a need to communicate." She believed that the Smith family members communicate without speaking. For example, emotion shows on her face.

What effect did Dr. Reynolds's presence have on the family?

"It was enjoyable," Charles, Sr., replied.

Jewel went on, "David fitted in. We were a little tense at first—had to feel him out. We've been around young people a lot; if David were older and finicky, then maybe there'd have been a problem."

"It was interesting at first, like a guest—hospitable—then he was like a member of the family," Chuck remarked. "Sometimes I felt I had to watch myself—someone was recording what I did—but I soon became used to it."

"It goes back to our kids' childhood," Mrs. Smith said. "Some young person was there at our home all the time."

Mr. Smith got up while Jewel was talking and stood in front of her to pick up some cigarettes and matches off the table. "Honey, that is so rude."

"I said I'm sorry."

Jewel thought that "his nerves" caused Chuck to go back to the hospital. She said she knew the day before that he would be going back to the hospital. "I've learned over the years to be able to tell."

Mr. Smith could tell two to three days ahead by Chuck's rocking back and forth.

"Were you aware of the rocking, Chuck?" his mother asked.

Chuck said that he was not aware until a social worker called his attention to it.

Another clue for Jewel was the way Chuck smoked cigarettes. She did not know why the tension built up. Chuck was "free as a bird here."

Chuck reasoned that he went back because the medication was not doing its job. Nothing out of the ordinary happened to him to provoke a relapse.

"But he lets it go too far before he tells them about it," Jewel noted.

Chuck replied that sometimes there were temporary downs, so he had to wait to see if he would recover spontaneously as he sometimes did.

Dr. Farberow inquired about Chuck's future.

"I just don't know," Jewel sighed.

Chuck thought that research would come up with a medicine with effects that would stay with him.

"I hope they do, I'll tell you." Jewel sounded weary. "We try to read all we can about it, to try to understand, to try to have hope."

"Do you feel discouraged?" Dr. Farberow asked.

"Sometimes I feel helpless," was Chuck's response.

"What would be helpful for readjustment?"

"Have someone like David live with the person," Mr. Smith offered.

"Depends on the individual," was Mrs. Smith's more cautious reply.

"What advice could you offer families of a discharged mental patient?"

Jewel replied, "Treat them as you've always treated them. . . . They can sense if you're putting on a front. It doesn't do any good to try to draw them out. When they're ready to talk, then listen."

"How do you react to a family member's decline?"

"I get tense. It's perfectly natural." Jewel shifted in her chair. She went on to say that she would like to see Chuck pay his one-third share of rent and expenses again.

"Chuck, how should a family behave when a patient returns home?"

"He should be accepted for what he is. Pressure him if necessary. If he can't live up to it, then he'll have to go back to the hospital."

"Were we okay?" Jewel wanted to know.

"Yes," Chuck reassured her.

"This is a good opportunity for us to talk with each other," Jewel smiled.

Chuck felt "guilty" about being in the hospital. He worried about job applications and about the stigma.

"It's something that can't be helped; it's done," Jewel suggested. "Either evade it or face it squarely. . . . Let's face it; it isn't going to be easy to get a job."

Chuck praised the hospital staff. "They treat you like a human being even though you're sick." He considered the best treatment in the hospital and at home was to act as one would with an ordinary, normal person.

Jewel believed that a lot of people who had mental disorders were not in hospitals. "Big business people—they know how to put on a front." She believed that Chuck was more sane than most politicians. Mr. Smith evaluated Chuck as sharper than Agnew and just as sane.

Jewel thought Chuck should be around people who give him confidence. His family could not do it. Chuck felt they were pushing him when they tried to help. "You can feel free to tell your innermost secrets to strangers because you'll never see them again," Chuck remarked spontaneously.

The high point of being home for Chuck had been during the first couple of weeks, then the schoolwork trouble had begun.

His father did not know Chuck had gone back to the hospital until he came home from work.

Jewel had told him. She had been upset and Mr. Smith had been sad. Each time when Chuck would first come home, Jewel would feel elated. Then she would become very depressed for two to three days before he went back.

Charles, Sr., expressed his belief that Chuck would be happier if he were making his own living. Mr. Smith would always take any sort of job until he could find something satisfactory. He implied that Chuck would not do such a thing.

Jewel predicted that Chuck would feel depressed and hurt during the first few instances of being turned down when job-seeking. She began speaking in self-praise of her rug and her reindeer Christmas decorations. She gave Chuck his completed afghan. He hugged and kissed her.

APPENDIX A

AUTHORIZATION BY PATIENT AND FAMILY FOR USE OF PROCEDURES FOR INVESTIGATIONAL PURPOSES

Name _____ Date _____

We, *the family of Charles Smith, Jr.,* agree to participate in a study which has as its objective the investigation of positive and negative life experiences of a patient during the first month following his discharge from a psychiatric hospital. We hereby agree to receive *Dr. David Reynolds* as a participant-observer within our family during the period from *February 20th* to *March 20th*. The nature and purpose of the procedure and the pertinent potential results have been explained to us by the investigators and we understand what is involved. Specifically, Dr. Farberow and Dr. Reynolds explained to us that Dr. Reynolds, an anthropologist, will take notes and tape recordings as he participates in Charles's daily activities, including those activities within the family. We understand that, if we desire to do so, we are free to read Dr. Reynolds's notes, to listen to the taped material, and to offer our interpretations of the recorded events. We have been told that we will be offered structured assessments of our family that we may participate in as our time and interest permit.

We recognize that our family's identity will be protected and that in any published material we will remain anonymous. We understand that the results of this research will be of potential benefit in preparing other psychiatric patients for return to family and community life.

We understand we will receive as payment for Dr. Reynolds's board the sum of $30.00 per week (or prorated) and a lump sum of *$300.00* at the termination of the month's stay with us.

AUTHORIZATION BY PATIENT AND FAMILY FOR
USE OF PROCEDURES FOR INVESTIGATIONAL PURPOSES
(continued)

We also agree not to hold the National Institute of Mental Health, the Veterans Administration and its staff, or the investigators in this study responsible or legally liable for any harm or injury or damage that may come to any member of our immediate family or household or to our property during the period of the investigator's stay with our family.

We acknowledge that while no guarantee or assurance has been made as to the results that may be obtained, since investigational results cannot be fully foreseen, nonetheless the investigators will take every precaution consistent with the best investigative practice, and that our participation in this study may prove of benefit to us and in advancing scientific knowledge.

_____
Patient's Signature

_____
Family Member's Signature

_____
Principal Investigator

APPENDIX B

INTERPERSONAL CHECKLIST

Every family member (along with the anthropologist) filled out a Leary Interpersonal Checklist describing all the family members. The checklist consists of a series of descriptive words and phrases related to character traits such as self-respecting, bossy, easily embarrassed, often helped by others, jealous, meek, likes to be taken care of, and so forth. Beside each character trait, each family member was instructed to write the initial of every family member (including himself) who possessed that trait. If the description applied to no one in the family, it was left blank. The results were tabulated and summarized as follows:

Four or five other raters agreed that Charles, Sr., could be described as: Likes responsibility, self-respecting, self-confident, self-reliant and assertive, firm but just, stern but fair, can be frank and honest, able to doubt others, appreciative, considerate, helpful, well thought of, respected by others, able to take care of self.

Four or five other raters agreed that Jewel could be described as: Likes responsibility, self-respecting, self-confident, self-reliant and assertive, somewhat snobbish, hard-boiled when necessary, can complain if necessary, able to criticize self, well thought of, respected by others, able to take care of self, can be frank and honest, outspoken, able to doubt others, appreciative, cooperative, encouraging others, kind and reassuring, affectionate and understanding, sociable and neighborly, bighearted and unselfish.

Four or five other raters agreed that Leon could be described as: Independent, can complain if necessary, appreciative.

Four or five other raters agreed that Chuck could be described as: Able to give orders, often gloomy, able to criticize self, lacks self-confidence, very respectful to authority, well thought of, can be frank and honest, can be obedient, appreciative, wants everyone to like him, considerate, affectionate and understanding, helpful, big-hearted and unselfish.

Four or five other raters agreed that Donna could be described as: Self-respecting, independent, self-confident, self-reliant and assertive, can complain if necessary, well thought of, makes a good impression, respected by others, able to take care of self, likes to compete with others, can be frank and honest, able to doubt others, very anxious to be approved of, eager to get along with others, encouraging others, affectionate and understanding, sociable and neighborly, bighearted and unselfish.

Charles, Sr., rated himself as having these qualities, but no one else did: tries to be too successful, encouraging others, tries to comfort everyone, enjoys taking care of others, gives freely of self. Apparently he saw himself as more nurturant than others did. Jewel rated herself as having these qualities but no one else did: selfish, slow to forgive a wrong, and oversympathetic. Chuck rated himself as having these qualities but no one else did: Impatient with others' mistakes, admires and imitates others, acts important, selfish, frequently disappointed. Donna rated herself as having these qualities but no one else did: forceful, dictatorial, boastful, somewhat snobbish, egotistical and conceited, can be strict if necessary, impatient with others' mistakes, self-seeking, sarcastic, often gloomy, complaining, critical of others, frequently disappointed, wants everyone's love, forgives anything, likes everybody, loves everyone.

Three or more other raters found this quality in Charles, Sr., but he did not: likes responsibility, can be strict if necessary. Three or more other raters found this quality in Jewel, but she did not: able to give an order, dominating, proud and self-satisfied, can be strict if necessary, dependent, critical of others, able to doubt others, can be obedient, cooperative, kind and reassuring, friendly, helpful, enjoys taking care of others. Three or more other raters found this quality in Chuck, but he did not: self-respecting, can complain if necessary, able to criticize self, apologetic, lacks self-confidence, grateful, often helped by others, very respectful to authority, dependent, well thought of, respected by others, able to doubt others, very anxious to be approved of, likes to get along with others, affectionate, bighearted and unselfish.

There were several characteristics in family members that the researcher perceived but no one else seemed to see. This discrepancy may represent family blind spots, researcher bias, or both. Reynolds saw Charles, Sr., as forceful, sarcastic, acts important, likes to compete with others, and stubborn. He saw Jewel as dependent, likes to compete with others, and frequently disappointed. He saw Chuck as bitter, resentful, and timid. And he saw Donna as dominating.

A crude measure of projection, or, alternatively interpreted, of important dimensions of evaluation, was found by totaling the number of ratings each rater made for all family members and combining these in a class of characteristics. For example, for all eight characteristics related to *meekness*, Jewel made only three ratings. But she found the descriptions of the eight characteristics related to *self-esteem* much more applicable to family members, and she made eighteen ratings in that class. The classes most frequently used by Charles, Sr., Jewel, Donna, and Reynolds were the same: *self-esteem* and *other-directed*. Chuck used no class of descriptions more than others. The anthropologist used a third class the most frequently, that of *dominance*.

BIBLIOGRAPHY

Alanen, Yrjo O. *The Mothers of Schizophrenic Patients.* Copenhagen: Ejnar Munkstaardt, 1958.

Bateson, Gregory, Jackson, Don D., Haley, Jay, and Weakland, John. Toward a theory of schizophrenia. *In* Buss, Arnold H. and Buss, Edith H. (eds.). *Theories of Schizophrenia.* New York: Atherton Press, 1969.

Beels, C. Christian. Family and social management of schizophrenia. *Schizophrenia Bulletin*, no. 13:97-118 (Summer) 1975.

Bell, N., and Vogel, E. F. *The Family.* Glencoe, Ill.: The Free Press, 1960.

Blatt, Sidney, and Wild, Cynthia M. *Schizophrenia: A Developmental Analysis.* New York: Academic Press, 1976.

Bowen, Murray. A family concept of schizophrenia. *In* Jackson, Don D. (ed.). *The Etiology of Schizophrenia.* New York: Basic Books, 1960.

Buss, Arnold H., and Buss, Edith H. (eds.). *Theories of Schizophrenia.* New York: Atherton Press, 1969.

Clark, Alfred W., and Cullen, William S. Social support: A counter to pathogenic communication. *Interpersonal Development*, 5(1):50-59, 1974-1975.

Clausen, John A., and Kohn, Melvin L. Social relations and schizophrenia: A research report and perspective. *In* Jackson, Don D. (ed.). *The Etiology of Schizophrenia.* New York: Basic Books, 1960.

Evans, Anne S., and Bullard, Dexter M. The family as a potential resource in the rehabilitation of the chronic schizophrenic. *Mental Hygiene*, 44:64-73, 1960.

Farberow, Norman L., Ganzler, Sidney, Cutter, Fred, and Reynolds, David K. An eight-year survey of hospital suicides. *Life-Threatening Behavior*, 1(3): 184-202, 1971.

Faris, Robert E. L. Cultural isolation and the schizophrenic personality. *In* Buss, Arnold H., and Buss, Edith H. (eds.). *Theories of Schizophrenia.* New York: Atherton Press, 1969. First published *American Journal of Sociology*, 40:155-164, 1934.

Feldman, H. Communicative aspects of studies in schizophrenia. *Psychiatria Clinica*, 8(5):250-265, 1975.

Frank, Sheldon M., Allen, Doris A., Sleen, Lorrayne, and Myers, Beverly. Linguistic performance in vulnerable and autistic children and their mothers. *American Journal of Psychiatry*, 133(8):909-915, 1976.

Freeman, Richard V., and Grayson, Harry M. Maternal attitudes in schizophrenia. *Journal of Abnormal and Social Psychology*, 50:45-52, 1955.

Friedman, Alfred S. Symposium: Family treatment of schizophrenia. Family therapy as conducted in the home. *Family Process*, 1(1):133-140, 1962.

Friedman, Alfred S., Boszormeny-Nagy, Ivan, Jungreis, Jerome E., Lincoln, Geraldine, Mitchell, Howard E., Sonne, John C., Speck, Ross V., and Spivak, George. *Psychotherapy for the Whole Family*. New York: Springer Publishing Co., 1965.

Fromm-Reichman, Frieda. Transference problems in schizophrenia. *Psychoanalytic Quarterly*, 8:412-426, 1939.

Garmezy, Norman, and Rodnick, Elliot H. Premorbid adjustment and performance in schizophrenia: Implications for interpreting heterogeneity in schizophrenia. *Journal of Nervous and Mental Disease*, 129:450-466, 1959.

Gerard, D. L., and Siegel, J. The family background and schizophrenia. *Psychiatric Quarterly*, 24:47-73, 1950.

Goldman, Alfred E. A comparative-developmental approach to schizophrenia. *In* Buss, Arnold H., and Buss, Edith H. (eds.). *Theories of Schizophrenia*. New York: Atherton Press, 1969. First published *Psychological Bulletin*, 59:57-69, 1962.

Henry, Jules. *Pathways to Madness*. New York: Random House, 1965.

Kantor, R. E., and Winder, C. The process-reactive continuum: A theoretical proposal. *Journal of Nervous and Mental Disease*, 129:429-434, 1959.

King, Peter D. Early infant autism: Relation to schizophrenia. *Journal of the American Academy of Child Psychiatry*, 14(4):666-682, 1975.

Laing, R. D. Mystification, confusion, and conflict. *In* Boszormeny-Nagy, I., and Framo, J. L., *Intensive Family Therapy: Theoretical and Practical Aspects*. New York: Harper and Row, 1965.

Laing, R., and Esterson, A. *Sanity, Madness and the Family*. London: Tavistock Publications, 1964.

Lerner, Paul M. Resolution of intrafamilial role conflict in families of schizophrenic patients, II. Social maturity. *Journal of Nervous and Mental Diseases*, 145(4):336-341, 1968; *Dissertation Abstracts*, 25(11,12):6761-6762, 1969.

Lidz, Theodore. The intrafamilial environment of the schizophrenic patient, I. The father. *Psychiatry*, 20:329-342, 1957.

————. *The Origin and Treatment of Schizophrenic Disorders*. New York: Basic Books, 1973.

Lidz, Theodore, Fleck, Stephen, and Cornelison, Alice R. *Schizophrenia and the Family*. New York: International Universities Press, 1965.

Mark, J. C. The attitudes of mothers of male schizophrenics toward child behavior. *Journal of Abnormal and Social Psychology*, 48:185-189, 1953.

McGhie, Andrew, and Chapman, James. Disorders of attention and perception in early schizophrenia. *In* Buss, Arnold H., and Buss, Edith H. (eds.). *Theories of Schizophrenia*. New York: Atherton Press, 1969. First published *British Journal of Medical Psychology*, 34:103-117, 1961.

Mednick, Sarnoff. A learning theory approach to research in schizophrenia. *Psychological Bulletin*, 55:316-327, 1958.

Meehl, Paul E. Schizotaxia, schizotypy, schizophrenia. *In* Buss, Arnold H., and Buss, Edith H. (eds.). *Theories of Schizophrenia*, New York: Atherton Press, 1969. First published *American Psychologist*, 17:827-838, 1962.

Mishler, Elliot G., and Waxler, Nancy E. *Interaction in Families*. New York: John Wiley and Sons, 1968.

Prout, C. J., and White, Mary A. A controlled study of personality relationships in mothers of schizophrenic male patients. *American Journal of Psychiatry*, 107:251-256, 1950.

Reiss, David. The family and schizophrenia. *American Journal of Psychiatry*, 133(2):181-189, 1976.

Reynolds, David K., and Farberow, Norman L. *Endangered Hope: Experiences In Psychiatric Aftercare Facilities*. Berkeley, Los Angeles, London: University of California Press, 1977.

————. *Suicide: Inside and Out*. Berkeley, Los Angeles, London: University of California Press, 1976.

Rodnick, Elliot, and Garmezy, Norman. *In* Jones, Marshall R. (ed.). *Nebraska Symposium on Motivation*. Lincoln: University of Nebraska Press, 1957.

Rogler, Lloyd H., and Hollingshead, August B. *Trapped: Families and Schizophrenia*. New York: John Wiley and Sons, 1965.

Suzuki, Koji. A study of families of schizophrenic patients: A study utilizing the family consensus Rorschach. *Journal of Mental Health*, 46(20):1-40, 1972.

Takatomi, Takeshi, Suzuki, Koji, and Dendo, Hisako. A study of families of schizophrenic patients, II. Difference between the characteristic features found in the parent of male patients and those of female patients. *Journal of Mental Health*, 46(20):41-76, 1972.

Umbarger, Carter, and Hare, Rachel. A structural approach to patient and therapist disengagement from a schizophrenic family. *American Journal of Psychiatry*, 27(2):274-284, 1973.

Waring, E. M. Family therapy and schizophrenia. *Canadian Psychiatric Association Journal*, 23:51-58, 1978.

Wender, P., Rosenthal, D., Zahn, T., and Kety, S. The psychiatric adjustment of the adoptive parents of schizophrenics. *American Journal of Psychiatry*, 127:1013-1018, 1971.

Winter, David A. Some characteristics of schizophrenics and their parents. *British Journal of Social and Clinical Psychology*, 14(3):279-290 (September) 1975.

Wynne, Lyman C., Rykoff, Irving M., Day, Juliana, and Hirsch, Stanley I. Pseudomutuality in the family relations of schizophrenics. *Psychiatry*, 21(2):205-220 (May) 1958.

Wynne, Lyman C., and Singer, Margaret T. Thought disorder and family relations of schizophrenics, II. A classification of forms of thinking. *Archives of General Psychiatry*, 9:199-206, 1963.

INDEX